VICTORY
HOW WOMEN WON IT

Victory!

VICTORY
HOW WOMEN WON IT

A Centennial Symposium
1840-1940

By

The National American
Woman Suffrage Association

THE H. W. WILSON COMPANY
NEW YORK   1940

Copyright 1940
By The H. W. Wilson Company

All Rights Reserved

Published October 1940

PRINTED IN THE UNITED STATES OF AMERICA

Dedication

This book is based upon the records and has been prepared under the auspices of the National American Woman Suffrage Association, lineal descendant of those pioneers who first conceived the idea of uniting in order to take collective action to remedy their grievances, and is by it dedicated to the Women of the United States in whose behalf the labor of one hundred years was expended.

Foreword

A resume of the outstanding accomplishments of a century should prove useful to those who read or conduct research and for that purpose this book is written.

The century from 1840 to 1940 may appropriately be called the Woman's Century. That term was once applied by Victor Hugo to another period, but the events of that time did not fit the title, and his Century had no beginning nor end. This one is complete. In 1840 for the first time women proposed to unite, organize and to remove their grievances. In 1940 this aim with slight exceptions has been achieved.

In all the days of history no century brought to men so many rights and so much freedom as this hundred years has brought to women. It was not a peaceful period. One hundred and twenty-eight wars between nations were fought within the century, many extending over four years. Yet in the Woman's Campaign no blood was shed, no lives were lost, and no votes bought or sold. Reason, logic, patience, determination, union—these were the weapons which won the final victory. There is much to be learned from the Woman's Campaign by those who would use the same weapons for future battles for the right.

At this moment Democracy is being questioned, criticised and condemned. The world is being invited to choose between governments by the people aiming to promote their own welfare and totalitarian forms where one man or a limited group decides what is best for the many.

FOREWORD

Two pertinent questions arise from the American woman suffrage campaign over which thoughtful citizens may well ponder. The history, traditions and constitution of this country indicated that universal suffrage was inevitable. More, there was nothing in the United States to fear from women, for they were in minority. In no other country did history or tradition point to woman suffrage as inevitable and in most of them women were in majority.

1. Why then were women forced to labor without pause for seventy-two consecutive years to get the vote?
2. Why did it happen that even then twenty-six countries had given votes to their women before this nation did?

Why? Because Democracy failed. It did not continue to march forward under the old banner of the Rights of Man. It lay down and let come what would, and what did come was the totalitarians! Chiefly they arose in the great cities where a dictator, usually called a Boss, led them. The men were paid for their loyalty by cash, jobs or favors. They were in large part newcomers, ignorant and with no understanding of democracy. The Boss threw votes by the thousand into his party's till. These totalitarian spots in our country belonged to no one party. It was democratic in New York and republican in Philadelphia; many cities had their totalitarian groups. At times they controlled states, and votes in Legislatures and the Congress were bought and sold. The old American spirit degenerated. Liberty and freedom were mere oratorical words. The Bill of Rights had become meaningless. At last, tired and not a little disillusioned, women won the vote.

FOREWORD

Corruption has been lessened but its possibilities are not destroyed. No wonder the "Fifth Column" arouses fear. The same insidious enemy has been here before, under another name, and it nearly demolished the Republic. We are now not so much in need of war-ships and bombs for defense as of men and women who uphold a positive democracy and are citizens confident and unafraid. Our danger lies in ignorant, dishonest men and women and weasel-minded lookers on. The woman suffrage story demonstrated how such citizens may check progress, misrepresent facts and defeat justice without comprehending what they do.

The pioneers laid down a program in 1848 which the women of this country have faithfully followed. As a gift from the Woman's Century, equipped with education, self respect, self reliance, courage, understanding and armed with the vote, this nation now has an army of a new variety of women. What now, women of America! Alas there can be no pause. Another century calls you. Side by side with men-citizens it is for you to rejuvenate the Republic, revivify its faith and replenish the fires of human freedom. There is room on this round earth for all humans. There is food, clothing and shelter enough to make all comfortable. There should be freedom enough to enable every soul to grow and to live the life for which it yearns.

The next century must disclose what liberty really means, how it may be preserved in order that it may benefit the entire human race. With the same consecration to a great cause manifested by the pioneers who set our feet upon the path leading upwards, with the same devotion

FOREWORD

revealed by those who came after and performed the drudgery of weary years, will you, free women of America, lead on to that ideal democracy never yet attained, but which alone can salvage threatened civilization?

CARRIE CHAPMAN CATT

Contents

Chapter

I	PRELIMINARY AGITATION	1
	Mary Foulke Morrisson	
II	FIRST ORGANIZED ACTION	13
	Mary Gray Peck	
III	RAMPANT WOMEN	33
	Mildred Adams	
IV	"THAT WORD MALE"	47
	Mary Foulke Morrisson	
V	WYOMING: THE FIRST SURRENDER	57
	Carrie Chapman Catt	
VI	CAMPAIGNING STATE BY STATE	69
	Maud Wood Park	
VII	THE OPPOSITION BREAKS	81
	Gertrude Foster Brown	
VIII	APPEALS TO CONGRESS	95
	Penelope P. B. Huse	
IX	A DECISIVE VICTORY WON	105
	Gertrude Foster Brown	
X	THE WINNING PLAN	121
	Maud Wood Park	
XI	THE SECRETARY HAS SIGNED THE PROCLAMATION ..	141
	Mary Gray Peck	

CONTENTS—*continued*

Appendix

Bibliography 155
The National American Woman Suffrage Association 157
Interesting Events in the Woman Movement 159
The Electoral Thermometer 161
Partial Suffrage Gains 165
Directions for State Work in Supporting 19th Amendment ... 167
Directions for Lobbyists 170
Chronology of Congressional Action 172
Authors Who's Who 173

Illustrations and Biographies

                                                      FOLLOWS PAGE

FRONTISPIECE

LUCRETIA COFFIN MOTT 20

LUCY STONE 42

ELIZABETH CADY STANTON 64

SUSAN B. ANTHONY 90

ANNA HOWARD SHAW 104

SPEAKER GILLETT OF THE HOUSE OF REPRESENTATIVES SIGNS SUFFRAGE BILL JUNE 5, 1919 124

CARRIE CHAPMAN CATT 146

Chapter I
Preliminary Agitation
Mary Foulke Morrisson

Chapter I

Preliminary Agitation

"I long to hear that you have declared an independency, and, by the way, in the new code of laws which I suppose it will be necessary for you to make, I desire that you should remember the ladies and be more generous and favorable to them than your ancestors. . . . If particular care and attention are not paid to the ladies we are determined to foment a rebellion, and will not hold ourselves bound to obey any laws in which we have no voice or representation."

So wrote Abigail Adams to John in 1776 when he was attending the Continental Congress. This was almost the first gun fired in a campaign that was to take sixty years for its formal declaration and eighty more for victory.

Today men and women are equal politically. There are but few legal inequalities. The most advanced training, academic and technical, is open to women. They work in factories, in business, in government offices, in the professions, not always welcome, not always on equal terms with men, but taken for granted as a functioning part of our economic structure. Consider these facts and then look back only one hundred years when the woman's rights movement was in its derided beginnings.

Its history, briefly outlined in this volume, does not lessen the wonder that a tiny handful of heroic pioneers could have brought about so profound a change in the fundamentals of American life. They started an eighty-year crusade, eighty years of slogging persistence, high courage and resourceful statesmanship. In spite of abuse and betrayal not one act of violence marred their long effort. They could not compel the granting of these rights, they could only appeal to the sense of justice of American men to make democracy complete. And the men responded.

In these days, when force seems the only law; when, as Lenin says, "Liberty must be rationed"; with dictators on the march and the old liberal ideals trampled under foot, we do well to read the story again to confirm our faith in the democratic processes. If a handful could bring about so tremendous a reform surely we need not despair. Let us see how far we have come, we to whom freedom is so much a matter of course that we have already forgotten how short a time it has been ours, how hardly won.

In the early days of the 19th century according to the common law of England and of the United States, "husband and wife were one and that one the husband." A married woman was said to be "dead in law." A man had absolute power over his children; controlled his wife's property, could collect and spend her wages and beat her "with a stick no bigger than the judge's thumb." This prerogative was exercised. We read of a worthy Methodist class leader who used a horsewhip on his wife every few weeks "to keep her in subjection because she scolded too much." [Massachusetts was the only state that forbade wife-beating.]

The husband owned the wife's person. If she ran away, no matter what the provocation, he could compel her return and collect damages from the person who gave her shelter—"harboring" they called it. If a wife were injured in an accident the husband sued for damages for the loss of her services. No damages were due her if he were incapacitated. Of course there were many fine men who treated their wives with kindness, sometimes with respect, but there was no legal recourse against unjust or brutal husbands, and the doctrine of the divine right of men to rule over women was believed by nearly everybody, even by those who had had a large part in upsetting the equally old doctrine of the divine right of kings. As for unmarried women, they were "old maids," dependent on their nearest male relative and the chores were assumed to be their natural portion.

No colleges were open to women, no high schools. A few private schools taught the three R's and accomplishments to the daughters of the rich. The poor went without learning. Here and there bold spirits said they thought the new public schools should be large enough for both boys and girls, and there was a storm of protest on the still familiar ground of economy. Then girls were allowed to come during the summer months while the boys worked on the farms, or after school hours in winter time.

Back in 1762 Rousseau, in "Emile" had stated with absolute frankness the then popular view of woman's sphere, a view that was long in dying. "The education of woman should always be relative to that of man. To please us, to be useful to us, to make us love and esteem them, to educate us when young, to take care of us when grown, to advise us, to console us, to render our lives easy and agreeable, these are the duties of women at all times and what they should be taught from their infancy."

There were, however, at long intervals, signs of a coming change. Count Zinzendorf when he came to America in 1742 at once founded a school for Moravian girls. By 1800 this had become a noted seminary and is today the Moravian College for Women. It was in 1790 that Mary Wollstonecraft threw down her challenge "I insist that not only the virtues but the knowledge of the two sexes should be the same, in nature if not in degree," for which and similar sentiments Horace Walpole called her a "hyena in petticoats." Yet in small corners where this shocking lady had never been heard of there were stirrings. In Gloucester, Massachusetts, also in 1790, the town fathers decided that "females are a tender and interesting branch of the Community but have been much neglected by the Public Schools of this town."

The only group that gave its women equality with men was the Quakers. Their women had not only an equal voice in church management but could speak with authority as ministers. Girls had the same education as boys, but even here the universal custom prevailed of paying women teachers only half as much as men—though the tuition for boys and girls was the same. Her sense of outrage at this injustice had its share in starting sixteen year old Lucretia Mott, a teacher at Nine Partners School, on her lifelong battle for equality of treatment for women.

Emma Willard in 1819 presented to the New York legislature her "Plan for Improving Female Education," and in 1821 opened her famous Female Seminary at Troy. A great step forward was taken by John J. Shipherd, twelve years later, in the founding of Oberlin, the first coeducational college in the United States. He listed in his circular among the prominent objects of the seminary "The elevation of female character by bringing within the reach of the misjudged and neglected sex all the instructive privileges which hitherto have unreasonably distinguished the leading sex from theirs."

Mary Lyon was planning for Mt. Holyoke about this time, and found herself handicapped by not being able to get at her object directly. Etiquette required a woman to be seen and not heard. It was, she said, better to have the scheme appear to originate with men, otherwise many good men would fear the effect on society of so much female influence. Dr. Gregory's popular "Legacy to My Daughters" published some thirty years before, was evidently still up-to-date. He had written, "If you happen to have any learning keep it a profound secret, especially from men, who look with a jealous, malignant eye on a woman of great parts and cultivated understanding."

The movement for the emancipation of woman began in earnest when a few heroic souls dared to speak from public platforms in behalf of causes in which they believed. Two young South Carolina women, Sarah and Angelina Grimké, who knew at first hand what slavery meant, freed their own slaves and came north to preach against the system. They started at parlor meetings of church-women, but they were so gifted, courageous and eloquent and knew so well whereof they spoke that no parlor could hold the women and men who thronged to hear them and the meetings moved to the churches. When a committee of the Massachusetts legislature met in 1838 to consider anti-slavery petitions they invited Angelina to speak to them, the first time a woman had been heard in the Boston State

House. Anti-slavery forces grew alarmed and stormed at the wickedness of allowing women to speak in public. Angelina wrote "We have given great offense on account of our womanhood, which seems to be as objectionable as our abolitionism. The whole land seems roused to a discussion of the province of women and I am glad of it."

At the dedication of Pennsylvania Hall, in Philadelphia, built in 1837 chiefly by abolitionists to give a forum for "free discussion of all topics not immoral," Angelina Grimké was among those speaking against slavery. A mob gathered and she spoke to jeers and howls without, while stones crashed through the windows. After a superb exposition of the evils of slavery she asked "What is a mob? What would the breaking of every window be? What would the levelling of this hall be? Any evidence that we are wrong or that slavery is a good and wholesome institution? No!" The mob set fire to the hall and burned it to the ground but not till she had finished.

Abby Kelley, the most persecuted of the pioneers, made her first speech at that meeting. She gave to the anti-slavery cause all her small inheritance and devoted herself entirely to the work. She was preached against as a Jezebel, ostracized, often mobbed, and many who listened to her were expelled from their churches. She lectured in North Brookfield and Lucy Stone taught there, which is quite enough, even without the Grimké sisters, to account for the Pastoral Letter issued by the influential Massachusetts Conference of Congregational Ministers in 1837 against "those who encourage females to bear an obtrusive and ostentatious part in measures of reform, and countenance any of that sex who so far forget themselves as to itinerate in the character of public lecturers and teachers," a proceeding leading to "degeneracy and ruin."

This intense opposition to any public activity on the part of women split the anti-slavery forces. When in 1840 Abby Kelley was appointed to a committee of the Massachusetts society eight ministers resigned in protest. A new organization was formed with men members only. Of this organization Lucy Stone wrote to her brother, "It pretends to endeavor to remove the yoke of bondage on account of color. It is actually summoning all its energies to rivet more fully the chains that have always been fastened upon the necks of women."

Perhaps the first to perceive that women must assure their own freedom of action before they could work for others was Lucy Stone. As a child, growing up on a New England farm, she early realized that the work women did was as hard as that of men, but that in spite of it they were treated as inferiors. The injustice rankled and when she came across such Bible texts as "Wives submit yourselves unto your husbands as unto the Lord" she—quite literally—wanted to die. Reconsidering, she made up her mind to go to college and read those texts in the original to find out if the Lord really had said anything so unfair. Her father believed in college for his sons, but he thought his daughter's desire crazy, and refused help. So she earned the money herself, picking fruit, teaching school, all at such pitifully low wages that it took till she was twenty-five to pay her way to Oberlin, the only college admitting women.

She had money only for "deck passage" across Lake Erie, sleeping on deck among horses and freight. Her father after three years relented and helped her, but till then she had earned her way, teaching in the preparatory department, and washing dishes at three cents an hour. She cooked her own food and fed herself at a cost of fifty cents a week. Somehow she found time for teaching a class of Negroes and, already determined to be a lecturer, she managed, unknown to the Ladies Board, which would certainly have stopped her, to get practice in debate. The college did not permit its women students to speak in public and when she won the honor of being chosen to write a commencement address, finding it was to be read by a professor, she refused to write it.

She gave her first woman's rights lecture the year that she was graduated, 1847, and started out as a speaker for an anti-slavery society. When rebuked for mixing her subjects she said, "I was a woman before I was an abolitionist." There were no suffrage societies and she had no backing, so she put up the posters for her meetings and took up collections to pay for the hall. All sorts of indignities were dealt her. She was a rosy, friendly little person, with a remarkably sweet voice, very disarming to those who expected a virago.

Growing up during the 30's was another woman destined to be one of the most influential leaders of the woman movement, Elizabeth Cady Stanton. Her father's words as he sat by her dead brother, "Oh, my daughter, would you had been a boy" started her while a child on the study of Greek and Latin. She would do what she could to make up to her father the son he had lost. His one comment on her attainment was, "You should have been a boy."

In his law office she saw women pleading for help under unjust laws. The young law students amused themselves feeding her indignation by reading her the worst laws they could find. She marked them and thinking they pertained only to her father's practice she planned to do away with them by cutting them out. When her father explained that the laws belonged to the whole state and could be altered only by the legislature he turned her toward her future path.

The first legal reforms to be seriously considered related to the property rights of married women. In 1836 Judge Hartell had argued before the New York legislature for protection of these rights. Ernestine Rose, a Polish exile and one of the early women lecturers, had petitioned in 1837 for such legislation but got only five signatures. Sentiment for it grew however, thanks to her work and that of others and was strongly reinforced by the thrifty Dutch farmers who greatly disliked having their savings dissipated by spendthrift sons-in-law.

When Robert Dale Owen was trying to amend the women's property act in Indiana a legislator protested violently on the ground that "a most essential injury would result to the endearing relations of married life. Give to the wife a separate interest in law and all those high motives which operate to restrain the husband from wrong doing will be in a great degree removed. Woman's power comes through a self-sacrificing spirit ready to offer up all her hopes upon the shrine of her husband's wishes." The first breach in the wall of masculine authority did not come for nearly a decade. In 1848 the New York legislature passed a bill introduced by Judge Fine of St. Lawrence, giving married women control of their own property. He had tried to secure his wife in the control of hers and found it impossible under the existing laws.

The prophetic events of the 20's and 30's, though in the light of what was to come they are impressive, were scattered and unorganized and the great mass of women were untouched by the possibilities opening before them. It was the next two decades that were to be made dramatic by the swift and widespread awakening of women and the prompt and bitter opposition to the whole woman movement.

Chapter II
First Organized Action
Mary Gray Peck

Chapter II

First Organized Action

The story begins innocently enough in the month of June, 1840, when the packet, "Montreal," sailing from New York to Liverpool, was becalmed off the southwest coast of England, and three impatient passengers took to a small boat and were put ashore at Torquay. Two of the three were a young couple on their wedding trip, Henry Stanton and Elizabeth Cady Stanton; the third was the anti-slavery candidate for President of the United States, James G. Birney. The two gentlemen were American delegates to the first World Anti-slavery Convention, which was about to open in London, and it was the bride who hustled them into the small boat in order that they might get there on time.

During the eighteen-day voyage, the bride had been diligently coached on the slavery question by the two delegates so that she might do them credit when questioned by the English. She in turn had been observing the presidential nominee and deriving considerable secret amusement from their association. He was a polished gentleman of the old school who kindly endeavored to bestow some polish upon her, feeling that she was altogether too free and easy for London. She played chess with him evenings, and asked what he had found wrong with her behavior during the day!

The little party hastened to London by coach and went to a "lodging house in Queen Street," the headquarters of the American delegates. The next day eight women delegates arrived, five of whom came from Philadelphia, led by Lucretia Mott, three from Boston, led by Ann Green Phillips, wife of Wendell Phillips. Wendell Phillips and George Bradburn, the latter formerly of the Massachusetts legislature, were likewise among the Boston delegates. William Lloyd Garrison and Nathaniel P. Rogers were delayed at sea. Had Garrison got there on time the woman movement might not have started in 1840, for he was the most famous figure in the anti-slavery movement and the convention would have hesitated to throw out his delegates in his presence.

It was apparent that a question which had split the anti-slavery forces in America was going to make trouble in the London convention. As long as women served as hewers of wood and drawers of water, their aid was welcomed by the most conservative abolitionists. But when in 1838, Garrison nominated Abby Kelley to a place on a committee of the Anti-slavery Society, thus recognizing woman's equal status in the organization, there was vehement objection and a part of the society seceded to form what was known as the New Organization. Among these seceders were James G. Birney and Henry Stanton—but it should be noted that this was before Henry had married Elizabeth Cady. Naturally, the New Organization sent only men delegates to London, while Garrison's society sent both men and women.

Now women delegates to a convention was something unheard-of in England, and when it was learned that eight women delegates were coming over from the American Anti-slavery Society, a shudder passed over the land from

Scapa Flow to Land's End. The eight were likened to a cloud of harpies descending upon the capital and there was hectic consultation as to how to deal with this new terror. When they arrived in London, the dignity and propriety of their manner, the fact that the celebrated Lucretia Mott and the Philadelphia group were in Quaker dress, above all, the fact that they carried exactly the same credentials as the husbands who in several cases accompanied them, discouraged any open attack on them until the convention assembled. Then at the opening session, the storm burst.

As soon as the preliminary formalities were over, Wendell Phillips moved that a committee on credentials draw up a list of delegates. At once a debate on the eligibility of women was precipitated which with little sweetness and less light took up the remainder of the day. Several American gentlemen from the New Organization had the bad taste to speak against the admission of their countrywomen, and one of them was Birney.

When Mrs. Stanton saw her late mentor on social amenities get up and tell how the American Anti-slavery Society had been disrupted "by the persistence of the friends of promiscuous female representation," her heart swelled with anger. When shortly afterward her husband, also a delegate from the New Organization, rose and spoke warmly in favor of admitting the women, she listened with poignant relief. Altogether it was a momentous day in the long life of Elizabeth Cady Stanton, a day of which she has left full record. The things that were said about woman and her place in the world by this assemblage of masculine reformers kindled a fire in her soul that never went out.

If you would realize what women have accomplished in the way of changing public opinion during the last hundred years, listen to what men were saying about them with public approval in the year 1840. Not all the speakers were adverse. Dr. Bowring, an Englishman, struck a kindly note; said he, "I look upon this delegation from America as one of the most interesting, most encouraging and most delightful symptoms of the times, and I cannot believe that we shall refuse to welcome gratefully the cooperation which is offered us."

The Rev. J. Burnet was untroubled by kindly inhibitions. He demanded that the women take their credentials back and withdraw, since it never had occurred to the British Anti-slavery Society that ladies could possibly consider that the invitation to a convention would include them! But if they would not withdraw, he was in favor of dissolving the convention rather than accept them as delegates! The Rev. Henry Grew of Philadelphia went the Rev. Burnet one better. Said he, the admission of women would not only be a violation of the customs of England, but of the ordinance of Almighty God! One of the delegates from Philadelphia was named Mary Grew and one wonders if she were any connection of the Rev. Henry. She went back home to become a leader in the woman's rights movement as long as she lived!

George Bradburn of the Massachusetts legislature, over six feet in height and with a voice of thunder, did not like the inclusion of the customs of England alongside the ordinance of Almighty God. "We are told," he roared, "that it would be outraging the customs of England to allow women to sit in this convention. I ask, gentlemen, if it be right to set up the customs and habits, not to say prejudices of Englishmen on this occasion as a standard for Americans and several other independent nations? What a misnomer to call this a World's Convention of Abolitionists when some of the oldest abolitionists in the world are denied the right to be represented in it by delegates of their own choice!"

George Thompson of England answered the objections of Rev. J. Burnet seriatim and summarized them thus: "It seems that the grand objection to woman's appearance among us is this, *that it would be placing them on a footing of equality with us!*" Then he paid impassioned tribute to the labors of women in the anti-slavery cause and challenged the convention to say they had not earned the right to be acknowledged.

Wendell Phillips made a thrilling plea for the women who sat pale and silent, his beloved wife among them, throughout the humiliating scene. "We cannot yield this question if we would," he cried, "for it is a matter of conscience. But neither would we yield it as a matter of expediency, for in doing so we should feel that we were striking off the right arm of our enterprise. We have argued it over and over again, and decided it time after time in favor of the women. We have not changed by crossing the water. We think it right for women to sit by our side there, and we think it right for them to do the same here. We ask the convention to admit them; if they do not choose to grant it, the responsibility rests on their shoulders, not on ours."

Rev. Eben Galusha of New York commended the example of England's noble Queen, "who by sanctioning her consort, Prince Albert, in taking the chair on an occasion not dissimilar to this, showed her sense of propriety in putting her Head foremost in an assembly of gentlemen. I have no objection to woman's being the neck to turn the head aright, but I do not wish her to assume the place of the head."

And so the debate went on until a late hour, some of the English clergy "dancing around with Bible in hand, shaking it in the face of the opposition," as Mrs. Stanton narrates. This spectacle so exasperated George Bradburn that he bellowed: "Gentlemen, prove to me that your Bible sanctions the slavery of women—the complete subjugation of one half of the race to the other half—and I should feel that the best work I could do for humanity would be to make a grand bonfire of every Bible in the universe!"

At this blasphemy, Rev. C. Stout could bear no more. He reminded the convention that it had assembled to do something about slavery, not to discuss "this paltry question." "Be men!" he cried. "Consider what is worthy of your attention!" The paltry question thereupon was put to vote, and the women who had come three thousand miles as regularly accredited delegates to a meeting in response to an official invitation, were refused recognition and shown to seats "behind the bar," separated by a low curtain from the delegate body.

Sitting in the gallery during this extraordinary scene were some of the most famous women in England. To show their displeasure they took every occasion to show courtesy to the American women. Harriet Martineau was too ill to be present, but she wrote Lucretia Mott expressing her shame at the indignity offered the American delegates.

Lucretia Mott.

Lucretia Coffin Mott

Lucretia Coffin was born on the Island of Nantucket, January 3, 1793. After her marriage to James Mott she moved to Philadelphia where she lived until her death November 11, 1880.

As a member of the Society of Friends she labored faithfully in the advocacy of their views and also for the abolition of slavery, the cause of temperance, the promotion of universal peace and the elevation of woman.

James and Lucretia Mott went to London in 1840 as delegates to the World's Anti-Slavery Convention. The convention refused to seat women delegates. This discrimination moved Lucretia Mott and Elizabeth Cady Stanton to lay plans to call, upon their return to America, a Woman's Rights Convention.

This first Woman's Rights Convention was convened in Seneca Falls, New York, in July 1848, "to discuss the social, civil and religious condition and rights of women."

From then on much of the indomitable energy of this slight, vivacious Quaker was dedicated to furthering women's rights, using her gift of eloquence aptly described by a contemporary as "Fullness of mind, warmth of heart, distinctness of utterance, facility of elucidation and vivacity of manner" to influence an ever widening audience. She was fearless in her approach, and her calmness and skill combined with her quiet humor, earnestness and dignity won many adherents.

At the Woman's Rights Convention in 1876, Lucretia Mott, then in her eighty-fourth year, presided over a session which broke up reluctantly after five hours. Mrs. Mott spoke again at the last Convention which she attended, in Rochester, New York in July, 1878.

Her clear logic, her keen analytical mind, her eloquence, and her healthy balance of good qualities were dedicated to the rights of humanity.

ANNA LORD STRAUSS
Great-Granddaughter of Lucretia Mott

Next day, when Garrison and Rogers arrived and learned what had taken place, they would not present their credentials or take any part in the meetings, and for the duration of the convention England beheld the spectacle of Garrison, the foremost figure in the abolition movement, looking down from the gallery in grim and silent condemnation of the conclave. "I can take no part in a convention which strikes down the most sacred rights of all women," he said through the press.

"That night," writes Mrs. Stanton, "as Mrs. Mott and I walked away, arm in arm, we resolved to hold a convention as soon as we returned home, and form a society to advocate the rights of women. At the lodging house the discussions at every meal were heated, and at last Mr. Birney packed his valise and sought more peaceful quarters." The new convert records with satisfaction that she found herself in "full accord with the ladies in combating most of the gentlemen. In spite of constant gentle nudgings by my husband under the table, and frowns by Mr. Birney opposite, the tantalizing tone of the conversation was too much for me to maintain silence."

For the first time in her life, Elizabeth was meeting men and women who believed in the equality of the sexes and it was a tremendous experience. "On one occasion," she continues, "we visited the British Museum with a large party, and on entering Mrs. Mott and myself sat down near the door to rest for a few moments, telling the party to go on, that we would follow. When they returned after an absence of three hours, there we sat in the same spot, having seen nothing but each other, wholly absorbed in questions of theology and social life."

Questions of theology were all-important in those days, especially to women, for, with honorable exceptions, theologians were opposed to woman's rights. The reason so many of the pioneers for equal rights were Quakers was that the Society of Friends never was theology-ridden. Men and women spoke and prayed with equal freedom and fervor in Quaker meetings; strict rules of conduct applied to men and women alike. It is easy to see that her friendship with Lucretia, coming as it did simultaneously with the exhibition of theological bigotry in the debate in the anti-slavery convention, should give Elizabeth Cady Stanton an anti-clerical bias, a bias which time did nothing to ameliorate, and which the clergy did considerable to strengthen!

On their return to America, the Stantons settled in Boston. The resolve to call a woman's rights convention was pushed into the background when Elizabeth found herself overwhelmed with the cares of a rapidly increasing family and an extraordinarily full and absorbing intellectual life. With Lucretia down in Philadelphia, also straining to keep abreast of the calls upon her, the two postponed although not forgetting their determination.

It was a time of passion and turmoil, of reforms and fairs to raise money for them; above all a time of conventions! These were not the calm affairs of today. They were free-for-alls, frequented by all who had an idea or a grievance to publish. When cranks insisted on monopolizing the time, they were forcibly carried to the door and set outside.

During these contentious years, women gradually took a more active part in reform movements. Margaret Fuller started her "conversations," informal lectures in private homes which were well attended by women. Ernestine Rose in her crusade for married women's property rights travelled over the eastern states and as far west as Wisconsin. Others agitated for temperance, anti-slavery, and peace, before audiences of women. Very slowly, legislation began to reflect a growing relaxation in the attitude toward women. Married women were given property rights between the years 1844 and 1848 by Maine, Mississippi, Pennsylvania and New York. Three young women were graduated from Oberlin College, first college to admit women, in 1841. Paulina Wright Davis was giving lectures on physiology, using a manikin to illustrate them, and women no longer fainted at the sight or even pulled down their veils as at first.

But it was not in Boston or New York or Philadelphia, where the ferment of ideas was liveliest, that the first big gun in the women's revolution was touched off. Of all the unlikely places, it was in Seneca Falls, New York, a country village on the Seneca River, with elm-shaded streets, half a dozen evangelical churches, beautiful limestone woolen and flour mills, and a state of mind compounded of the Shorter Catechism and Blacksone's Commentaries. Here the Stantons were living in the year, 1848, that year of revolutions in Europe, of Karl Marx and the Communist Manifesto, of deepening hostility between North and South in America over the new territory acquired after the Mexican War. But Seneca Falls was immune to revolutionary ideas—or so it thought. It disapproved of the radicalism of the neighboring town of Geneva, where a woman, Elizabeth Blackwell, had been permitted to enter the Medical College and dissect dead bodies, and thanked God that this could not have happened in Seneca Falls! Then the explosion came.

On a Friday morning of mid-July of this momentous year, Elizabeth Cady Stanton left her lively family of children at home and went to Waterloo, the county seat, five miles away, to spend the day at the home of Richard Hunt where Lucretia Mott and her sister, Martha Wright, were guests. Present also were the hostess, Jane Hunt, and Mary Ann McClintock. It was the first meeting for some years between Lucretia and Elizabeth, and the latter was deeply moved and poured out her thoughts to her adored friend with an impetuosity which stirred the circle indescribably. As they talked, their enthusiasm was communicated to the others, and they decided to call the long-delayed woman's rights convention in Seneca Falls the coming week. Forthwith they drew up the following call and sent it, unsigned, to the *Seneca County Courier* which published it.

"WOMAN'S RIGHTS CONVENTION—A Convention to discuss the social, civil and religious condition and rights of woman, will be held in the Wesleyan Chapel, at Seneca Falls, N.Y., on Wednesday and Thursday, the 19th and 20th of July current, commencing at 10 o'clock A. M. During the first day, the meeting will be exclusively for women, who are earnestly invited to attend. The public generally are invited to be present on the second day, when Lucretia Mott of Philadelphia, and other ladies and gentlemen will address the convention."

The fact that it was not signed is the only hint at trepidation in this call to a revolutionary assembly. There were only five days for preparation, and on Sunday morning, Mrs. Mott, Mrs. Wright and Mrs. Stanton met with Mary Ann

McClintock in the latter's parlor to draw up a Declaration of Sentiments and a set of resolutions to submit to the convention. The mahogany table on which these historic documents were written is now the chief object of interest in the Woman Suffrage collection in the Smithsonian Museum in Washington.

They worked all day with an ever growing realization of the magnitude of the task they had so lightly undertaken. When they attempted to crowd a complete thought into one concise expression, they were dismayed at the difficulty. They ransacked reports of men's conventions in search of models and were disgusted with the tameness and verbosity they found. Finally one of them thought of the Declaration of Independence, and read it aloud "with much spirit and emphasis." Here was the real thing! They set their teeth into the magnificent language of the resounding old charter with infinite satisfaction, and adopted it entire with some slight changes, "such as substituting 'All men' for 'King George' "!

In her graphic account of the day's work, Mrs. Stanton says:—"Knowing that women must have more to complain of than men under any circumstances possibly could, and seeing the Fathers had eighteen grievances, a protracted search was made through statute books, church usages, and the customs of society to find that exact number. Several well-disposed men assisted in their collecting, until with the announcement of the eighteenth, the women felt they had enough to go before the world with a good case."

Wednesday morning, July 19, 1848, came, and the four prime movers in the enterprise, carrying their Declaration and resolutions and an armful of law books for reference, repaired to the Wesleyan Chapel, where they found a crowd assembled and the door locked! An agile youth climbed through a window and unbarred the entrance, and the church was quickly filled. Perhaps because the call had stipulated that only women were invited to come the first day of the convention, a goodly proportion of men were on hand, filled with curiosity and more or less goodwill. There was a hasty consultation around the altar as to what to do about their presence. Mrs. Stanton records that the four who had called the meeting shrank from organizing and presiding over it, and decided that "this was an occasion when men might make themselves pre-eminently useful." It was agreed that they should remain and preside throughout the convention.

"James Mott, tall and dignified in Quaker costume, was called to the chair; Mary McClintock was appointed secretary. . . . Lucretia Mott, accustomed to public speaking in the Society of Friends, stated the objects of the convention, and in making a survey of the degraded condition of woman the world over, showed the importance of inaugurating some movement for her education and elevation. Mary McClintock and Mrs. Stanton each read a well-written speech. Martha Wright read some satirical articles she had published in the daily papers, answering the diatribes on woman's sphere. Ansel Bacon, who had been a member of the Constitutional Convention recently held in Albany, spoke at length on the property bill for married women, and the discussion on woman's rights in that convention. Samuel Tillman, a young student of law, read a series of the most exasperating laws for women. . . . The Declaration of Sentiments having been freely discussed was reread by Mrs. Stanton and with some slight amendments adopted."

Now in explanation of the nation-wide commotion stirred up by this first woman's rights convention, let us consider a few of its statements, clothed as they were in words familiar to every patriotic citizen, words he dared not challenge. That was one reason why he was so enraged!

"We hold these truths to be self evident: that all men and women are created equal; that they are endowed by their Creator with certain inalienable rights; . . . That to secure these rights governments are instituted, deriving their just powers from the consent of the governed. Whenever any form of government becomes destructive of these ends, it is the right of those who suffer from it . . . to insist upon the institution of a new government. . . . When a long train of usurpations and abuses . . . evinces a design to reduce them under absolute despotism, it is their duty to throw off such government, and to provide new guards for their future security.

"The history of mankind is a history of repeated injuries and usurpations on the part of man toward woman, having in direct object the establishment of an absolute tyranny over her. To prove this, let facts be submitted to a candid world."

Then come the grievances, foremost among them the denial of woman's inalienable right to the elective franchise. They cover the whole field of woman's inferior status—economic, political, social, domestic, religious—ending with these forthright words:

"Now in view of this entire disfranchisement of one half of the people of this country, their social and religious degradation—we insist that they have immediate admission to all the rights and privileges which belong to them as citizens of the United States. In entering upon the great work before us, we anticipate no small amount of misconception, misrepresentation and ridicule; but we shall use every instrumentality within our power to effect our object. . . . We hope this convention will be followed by a series of conventions in every part of the country."

With one exception, the resolutions which were proposed after the Declaration were passed without opposition. The exception was the one championed by Elizabeth Cady Stanton and Frederick Douglass, declaring that it "is the duty of the women of the country to secure to themselves the sacred right of the franchise." Even Lucretia Mott hesitated at that one. "Why Lizzie," she had pled, "Thee will make us ridiculous!" The convention likewise hemmed and hawed over it, but passed it by a small majority.

One hundred men and women signed the Declaration and resolutions, but when on the following Sunday, the whole country resounded with denunciations from the pulpit, when the press with a few exceptions heaped ridicule and abuse upon the meeting, the weak-kneed withdrew their names.

The business before the convention was not finished, and the meeting was adjourned to meet two weeks later in Rochester. Here Amy Post, who had attended the Seneca Falls convention, and Rhoda De Garmo insisted that a woman preside, and Abigail Bush was elected president. Mrs. Mott and Mrs. Stanton were so opposed to the idea that they threatened to depart homeward! However they were won over and Mrs. Bush was equal to her duties.

The opening speech of the president began thus: "Friends, we present ourselves here before you with trembling frames and faltering tongues, and we do not expect to be heard by all of you at first, but we trust that you will bear with our weakness in the infancy of the movement."

The apology was superfluous, for soon the gift of tongues descended upon them. Even the passing stranger got it! A bridal couple in transit through the city came to the convention, and the bride "asked the privilege of saying a few words, which was readily granted." Whereupon she held forth for twenty minutes, to the great delight of the rapt husband and the attentive audience. "It was a scene never to be forgotten," says Elizabeth Cady Stanton, and it certainly was a remarkable indication of the prevalence of unsuspected sympathy for the movement.

Sarah Owen's speech on women's wages gives a glimpse into the world of labor at that time. Said she, "An experienced cashier of this city remarked to me that women might be as good book-keepers as men, but men have monopolized every lucrative situation, from the drygoods merchant down to whitewashing. Who does not feel, as she sees a stout, athletic man standing behind the counter, measuring lace, ribbons and tape, that he is monopolizing a woman's place, while thousands of rich acres in our western world await his coming? ... I am informed by the seamstresses of this city that they get but thirty cents for making a satin vest, and from twelve to thirty for making pants. Man goes to a tailor and pays him double and even treble for making a suit, when it merely passes through his hands after a woman has made every stitch of it!"

There was general agreement on the principle of equal pay for equal work, but the gentlemen present were less complaisant when it came to a discussion of equality in the family. One man demanded to know who was to decide when the two heads of a family disagreed? Did not St. Paul enjoin obedience to husbands? Lucretia Mott replied that St. Paul was a bachelor; that no instance of trouble among the Society of Friends had arisen because the word, obedience, was omitted from the Quaker marriage contract. Other gentlemen wanted to know who should hold the property after marriage and if the husband should take the wife's name? Mrs. Stanton created a sensation when she replied to the last question "that in her opinion the custom of taking the husband's name was one main reason for woman's inferior status."

It will be seen from these fragmentary echoes of the Rochester adjourned meeting, that already the woman's rights cause had reached a state of free give and take in the arena of debate. The period of stage fright was past. The leaders had achieved confidence in their ability to answer and confound their opponents. Mrs. Stanton referred ironically to the Seneca Falls ministers who waited till the Sunday after the convention to criticise it, knowing that nobody would stand up in the congregation to dispute with them. The Seneca Falls Declaration and resolutions were formally adopted at Rochester and signed by many influential persons. While press and public remained hostile, they were unmistakably impressed with the assurance and completeness with which the women outlined their program. The virulence and extravagance with which its advocates were assailed bore eloquent testimony to the mental poverty of the assailants.

Similar conventions followed; in Ohio and the first truly national woman's rights convention in Massachusetts in 1850; Indiana, 1851; Pennsylvania, 1852. From that time on, the movement was organized on a national basis, speakers went out over the country, and the Woman's Rights Movement took its place among the great social struggles of the nineteenth and twentieth centuries.

The outstanding impression one gets in reviewing these beginnings is of the mental and moral stature of the Pioneers. They went with unerring instinct to the Declaration of Independence for their authority. They did not hesitate to range themselves alongside the greatest figures in American History,—who were also the wisest revolutionaries of whom the world has record,—when they claimed for women the great liberties the Fathers had achieved.

Chapter III

Rampant Women
Mildred Adams

Chapter III

Rampant Women

The ten years that struggled by between the first National Woman's Rights Convention in October 1850 and the seceding of South Carolina from the Union late in 1860 have as many names as there were facets to the rapidly expanding nation. It was the period of the Abolitionists and of that early temperance effort called the "Maine Law," of Transcendentalism in Massachusetts and a fever of railroad building in the West, of John Brown's raids, the Mormon migration, and the lining up of states for the Civil War that lay just ahead.

But in the story we are telling here, this decade was the reign of the "rampant women." The term was not meant to be as complimentary as it has now become. Invented by one of James Gordon Bennett's editorial writers, it appeared in the New York *Herald* of 1853 as comment on one of the many conventions for woman's rights.

"The assemblage of rampant women," said the paper, "which convened at the Tabernacle yesterday was an interesting phase in the comic history of the Nineteenth Century . . . a gathering of unsexed women, unsexed in mind, all of them publicly propounding the doctrine that they should be allowed to step out of their appropriate sphere to the neglect of those duties which both human and divine law have assigned them."

There might be more than one opinion concerning certain of these adjectives, but "rampant" the women certainly were. They had risen up from their church pews, their school-teacher benches, their parlor chairs, and they were standing erect on their own feet, avowedly out to secure their share of that liberty which was being so loudly cried as the American heritage. They had tried to speak for temperance, and found they first had to speak for a woman's right to open her mouth in public. They had tried to speak for the right of slaves to be free, and found that they had first to establish their own right to unmolested freedom of appearance on a public platform at an abolitionist meeting.

So by force of public pressure they came to the boiling point. If they were going to do effective work in school teacher assemblages, in churches, in sick rooms, for temperance, or for abolition of slavery, they must somehow get out from under these hampering insistences that their part in the world was to stay home and say nothing.

At an Anti-Slavery Convention in Boston in 1850 word was passed around that those interested in having a national woman's rights convention would meet in the ante room. Nine women stayed behind, and seven of them were appointed a committee to explore the possibilities. As Lucy Stone told it forty years later, "We talked the matter all over, and decided that it was time something was done for the women as well as for the Negroes, and that the best way to do it was to hold a convention. We did not know then how much cooperation we should have. The anti-slavery people were full of their own work, but Mr. Garrison, Wendell Phillips, Gerrit Smith, Henry C. Wright, and most of the abolitionists who were on the side of Mr. Garrison, were in favor of equal rights for women. We had not any money or any organization, and the question arose, How are we ever to make this woman's rights convention known? We agreed that we would divide the correspondence. Some would write to one State and some to another, to see whom we could get to unite in calling the convention."

By such simple methods, and with the help of men like William Lloyd Garrison and Wendell Phillips a call went out (in those days a call to a reform convention was a serious document with some pretension to literary merit) signed by eighty-nine men and women from six states. The convention was to be held "at Worcester, Mass., on the 23d and 24th of October next, to consider the question of Woman's Rights, Duties and Relations. The men and women who feel sufficient interest in the subject to give an earnest thought and effective effort to its rightful adjustment, are invited to meet each other in free conference at the time and place appointed."

It was an earnest age, and light language had as yet no place in great causes.

When the day came, more than a thousand men and women gathered in Brinley Hall, and Horace Greeley's New York *Tribune* reported that "if a larger place could have been had, many thousands more would have attended." They came from the six New England states, from New York, Pennsylvania, Iowa, Ohio, and far-away California—more than a third of the then Union. They came by stage coach, by river boat, by the new railroads with their hard seats which were just the same at night as in the daytime. The abolitionists were there, and the temperance people, two Negroes representing "the enslaved race," the Hicksite Quakers to whom both the Anthonys and the Motts belonged. So were the Boston Channings, Sargents, Parsons,

Wendell Phillips, an Alcott, Ralph Waldo Emerson. It was a meeting of earnest and liberal minds.

Because this was the first of the long series of national woman's rights conventions which extended, with some intermissions and variants, down to our own day, it is worth noting that William Henry Channing there suggested a plan for organizing the movement "for establishing woman's co-sovereignty with man." It was to have continuity from the beginning. A central committee was to be empowered to call conventions when and as it chose, and to keep in touch with other committees on education, industry, civil and political functions, social relations, and publications. The "next steps," recommended because "women alone can learn by experience and prove by works, what is their rightful sphere of duty," constituted a broad plan for action on which they speedily went to work.

Of the four women whose names were to become almost synonymous with agitation for women's rights in that part of the century, two—Lucretia Mott and Lucy Stone—attended that convention. Elizabeth Cady Stanton was busy having babies. Susan B. Anthony was taking care of the family farm near Rochester. She read the accounts of the convention in the *Tribune* and was much interested, but she was not yet quite convinced that equal rights included the suffrage.

Better than any other detail does that uncertainty of Miss Anthony's indicate how much had to be learned before the feminist ambitions of the forties and fifties were forced into the single channel of agitation for suffrage. Only after the Civil War did a few women become convinced that the right to vote was the key to all the others. Then a devoted handful settled down to the long, single-minded campaign that was finally to get results.

Of these four leaders among the rampant women of that day, Miss Anthony was the one whose campaigning became the most persistent. At the age of thirty-two, a confirmed spinster school-teacher and chafing under the narrow confines of her lot, she read the account of the Worcester convention. Two years later she met Elizabeth Cady Stanton at Seneca Falls, where she had gone to visit Amelia Bloomer. "There she stood," wrote Mrs. Stanton afterwards, "with her good earnest face and genial smile, dressed in gray delaine, hat and all the same color relieved with pale-blue ribbons, the perfection of neatness and sobriety. I liked her thoroughly from the beginning." Susan B. Anthony's school-teaching days were definitely over.

"We were at once fast friends," Mrs. Stanton wrote later, "in thought and sympathy we were one, and in the division of labor we exactly complemented each other. In writing we did better work together than either could alone. While she is slow and analytical in composition, I am rapid and sympathetic. I am the better writer, she the better critic. She supplied the facts and statistics, I the philosophy and rhetoric . . . and together we have made arguments that no man has answered. . . ."

The third of the indomitable trio was Lucy Stone. When in 1855 she married Henry Blackwell, it was with a ceremony that included a "Protest"—read aloud, signed, and widely circulated. After acknowledging their mutual affection the young pair "protest especially against the laws which give to the husband:

1. The custody of the wife's person.
2. The exclusive control and guardianship of their children.
3. The sole ownership of her personal property and use of her real estate, unless previously settled upon her, or placed in the hands of trustees, as in the case of minors, lunatics and idiots.
4. The absolute right to the product of her industry.
5. Also against laws which give to the widower so much larger and more permanent an interest in the property of his deceased wife than they give to the widow of the deceased husband.
6. Finally, against the whole system by which 'the legal existence of the wife is suspended during marriage' so that, in most states, she neither has a legal part in the choice of her residence, nor can she make a will, nor sue or be sued in her own name, nor inherit property."

What a furor this protest caused can be imagined even now. To the minds of most people it was little short of blasphemy. The ridicule and abuse which it brought down on the heads of the bride and groom was not lessened when it was learned that Lucy Stone did not intend to become Mrs. Henry Blackwell in the fashion of all other good wives, but would remain Lucy Stone.

The fourth great feminine figure of the fifties was an older woman, Lucretia Coffin Mott. Born of Quaker stock, married to James Mott in 1811, before any of the others were born, a Quaker preacher, a fearless and independent anti-slavery leader, it was her fine and reasonable conversation in the trying days of the London convention that played great part in hardening the resolution of the youthful Mrs. Stanton.

These women, together with Elizabeth Blackwell, the first woman doctor, Antoinette Brown, the first woman preacher, and others less famous but no less staunch, worked as individuals and in the group organized at Worcester. Mrs. Stanton describes their efforts during this period: "Night after night by an old-fashioned fireplace we plotted and planned the coming agitation, how, when and where each entering wedge could be driven, by which woman might be recognized and her rights secured. Speedily the state was aflame with disturbances in temperance and teachers' conventions, and the press heralded the news far and near that women delegates had suddenly appeared demanding admission in men's conventions; that their rights had been hotly contended session after session by liberal men on the one side, the clergy and learned professions on the other; an overwhelming majority rejected the women with terrible anathema and denunciations. Such battles were fought over and over in the chief cities of many of the northern states, until the bigotry of men in all the reforms and professions was thoroughly tested."

Digging back into the letters, the speeches, the yellowed newspaper clippings which tell what happened and how, perhaps the most difficult thing to understand is the kind of opposition the women aroused. So confident were they in the rightness of their cause, so reasonable does that cause seem now that its major objectives have been won and woven into the ordinary fabric of daily life, that it is very hard to give due weight to the frame of mind of the then majority. Yet all their work, their worry, and their eloquence will seem a kind of tilting at windmills unless it is recognized that these women were a small minority starting out to upset the established law and custom of a settled, not to say hide-bound, portion of the United States. They were agitating chiefly in New England, New York and Pennsylvania. They were attacking property laws, which were sacred then as now. They were demanding the extension of education, which costs money. In a society which prided itself on conforming to scriptural models, they were challenging the rule of biblical beliefs insofar as they referred to the proper place of woman.

These basic attacks on the established order of law and thought would have been in themselves enough to arouse sharp protest. In addition there was the further fact that these women were allied with other reform movements which were far from popular. Temperance was always a minority campaign. Abolition was by no means widely approved, and among conservative families there was even a strong aversion to the whole anti-slavery movement.

To these dubious causes some added from time to time agitation for clothes reform—in a day when long full skirts were synonymous with feminine virtue they insisted on wearing the Bloomer costume which was not only shorter but also bi-furcated; for rewriting of the Bible when the authority of the Scripture was challenged only by such a doubter as Charles Darwin. (The "Origin of Species" had just been published.) They held one or more meetings at water cures beloved of the hydrotherapists, and they were known to be friendly to the graduates of Brook Farm. It

Lucy Stone

Lucy Stone

Lucy Stone was born August 13, 1818, on a farm near West Brookfield, Mass. At Oberlin, Ohio, she organized the first debating society ever formed among college girls. She earned money towards her expenses by doing housework in the Ladies Boarding Hall at three cents an hour. She was graduated in 1847. She gave her first woman's rights lecture the same year. From 1847 to 1857 she lectured through the country to immense audiences. She was a small woman with gentle manners and a singularly sweet voice. She had great natural eloquence. Mobs would sometimes listen to her when they howled down every other speaker. She converted Susan B. Anthony, Julia Ward Howe, and Frances E. Willard to woman suffrage, as all three publicly testified. She headed the Call for the First National Woman's Rights Convention, held at Worcester, Mass. in 1850. On May 1, 1855, she married Henry B. Blackwell, keeping her own name, with his full approval. She took part in campaigns for State suffrage amendments, in Kansas 1867 and elsewhere and helped to organize a number of State Woman Suffrage Associations including that of Massachusetts. She was active in organizing the American Woman Suffrage Association and was chairman of its Executive Committee, and later of that of the National American Woman Suffrage Association. Her work was manifold for woman's education, property rights, etc. She raised most of the money with which the Woman's Journal was founded in Boston in 1870, and served on its editorial staff, first as an aid, later as editor till her death, October 18, 1893. A lifelong opponent said that up to that time the death of no woman in the United States had called out so widespread an expression of public affection and esteem.

ALICE STONE BLACKWELL
Daughter of Lucy Stone

was no wonder that the solid conservatives of the country rejected them with passion.

With these things in mind, the quantity and quality of the opposition they aroused becomes more understandable. They were thundered at from the pulpit; they were ridiculed in the press. The "rampant women" editorial was only one of many to point a scornful finger. They were excoriated by law-makers. In 1854, when a woman's rights petition with 5,931 signatures attached was presented to the New York legislature for action, a Mr. Burnett rose to speak against it. "It is well known," he said, "that the object of these unsexed women is to overthrow the most sacred of our institutions, to set at defiance the Divine Law which declares man and wife to be one, and establish on its ruins what will be in fact and in principle but a species of legalized adultery. . . . Are we to put the stamp of truth upon the libel here set forth, that men and women, in the matrimonial relation, are to be equal? We know that God created man as the representative of the race; that after his creation, his Creator took from his side the material for woman's creation; and that, by the institution of matrimony, woman was restored to the side of man, and became one flesh and one being, he being the head. But," he added with an almost pathetic fury, "this law of God and creation is spurned by these women."

Nevertheless, the indomitable ones persisted. Working in a time of agitation and confusion, sure of their ground, spurred on by a fervid conviction as to the rightness of their cause, they won extraordinary victories. In 1860 Susan B. Anthony, reporting to the Tenth National Woman's Rights Convention being held at Cooper Union in New York, said:

"Brave men and true . . . are now ready to help woman wherever she claims to stand. The press, too, has changed its tone. Instead of ridicule, we now have grave debate. And still more substantial praises of gold and silver have come to us . . . $400,000 from Mr. Vassar, of Poughkeepsie, to found a college for girls, equal in all respects to Yale and Harvard.

"During the past six years this state has been thoroughly canvassed, and every county that has been visited by our lecturers and tracts has rolled up petitions by the hundreds and thousands, asking for woman's right to vote and hold office—her right to her person, her wages, her children, and her home. Again and again have we held conventions at the capital, and addressed our legislature, demanding the exercise of all our rights as citizens of the Empire State. During the past year, we have had six women lecturing in New York for several months each. Conventions have been held in forty counties, one or more lectures delivered in one hundred and fifty towns and villages, our petitions circulated, and our tracts and documents sold and gratuitously distributed throughout the entire length and breadth of the State.

. . . The bills for woman's right to her property, her earnings and the guardianship of her children passed both branches of the legislature with scarcely a dissenting voice, and received the prompt signature of the governor."

Nor was New York state alone in this amazing progress. There was reason in Miss Anthony's triumphant declaration "And from what is being done on all sides, we have reason to believe that, as the Northern states shall one by one remodel their constitutions, the right of suffrage will be granted to women."

But Miss Anthony spoke too soon. The dawn was a false one. The next year, instead of an eleventh convention and further reports of progress came the secession of South Carolina and the start of a Civil War that was to put the women's cause back until the slave had been freed and national prohibition won.

Chapter IV

"That Word Male"
Mary Foulke Morrisson

Chapter IV

"That Word Male"

The work that women did during the Civil War when new and varied responsibilities were forced upon them, and the courage and ability with which they discharged those responsibilities did more to shatter the old ideals of woman's sphere than centuries of agitation could have done. Men were surprised and grateful and the women prepared to renew their campaign for the vote under what seemed happy auspices. To their dismay they found their cause inextricably mixed with the two red hot political questions, of what to do with the Negro and how to keep the Republicans in control of the Southern states. The 13th Amendment, freeing the slaves, had passed and was being ratified. Like a bolt from the blue in 1866, came the 14th Amendment, in which for the first time a citizen was defined as a male.

The problem before the Congress was of course difficult. Unless the Negro were protected in his rights as a citizen he would be and was being reduced to a state of peonage that was almost worse than slavery. Representation in the Southern states under the Constitution had been based on the number of white citizens and "three fourths of all other persons," which obviously required change. The enfranchisement of the Negro seemed necessary, and must be kept sharply distinct from so controversial a matter as woman suffrage.

Women were quick to point out how immeasurably worse off they would be if the amendment passed. Hitherto they had merely been in a class with children, idiots, criminals, now they were made the political inferiors of the race they had helped to free, a race still in the complete ignorance of slavery. Mrs. Stanton said further, (and her fear proved well founded), that unless women were enfranchised when the question of suffrage was strongly before the country, the tide of public interest would turn to other things, and could not easily be swung back. The women found, however, to their bitter disappointment, that the men who had been their staunchest friends, Charles Sumner, William Lloyd Garrison, Wendell Phillips, even Frederick Douglas, the Negro, all stood against them under the pretext, "This is the Negro's hour, the women's hour will come."

No woman's rights conventions had been held during the years of the war and the one which met in May, 1866 with the 14th Amendment then before Congress voted to resolve itself into the American Equal Rights Association; to work for suffrage for both women and Negroes, with Lucretia Mott as president and Henry Blackwell as recording secretary. When in 1869 the 15th Amendment came before the country the suffragists were divided. Sumner and the abolitionists felt that the Negro was entitled to the right of way. Lucy Stone, Mr. Blackwell and the majority of the American Equal Rights Association hoped the amendment might be extended to include women but that it must pass anyhow. Miss Anthony, Mrs. Stanton and a smaller group were willing to back it if it included women, but otherwise they opposed it. This brought down upon them fierce criticism from the abolitionists. The Association, torn by these divisions, split apart. Miss Anthony, Mrs. Stanton and their supporters organized the National Woman Suffrage Association in 1869 with a membership of women only. They still worked in the states wherever it seemed feasible, but they concentrated their main efforts on the Congress and introduced a woman suffrage amendment at every session. Lucy Stone, Henry Blackwell and their group later in the same year organized the American Woman Suffrage Association with the emphasis on state work since they felt that the Congress would not pay attention to women until there was a larger representation from states where women voted.

Two amendments to the state constitution had been before the Kansas voters in 1867. One struck the word "male" from the state constitution, the other the word "white." This was the first referendum on woman suffrage ever held (fifty-five were coming in the next fifty years) and eastern leaders were asked to help. Lucy Stone and Henry Blackwell worked several months, full of hope. When Miss Anthony and Mrs. Stanton came they enlisted the support of George Francis Train, a brilliant but erratic Democrat. He may have helped with the Democrats but he antagonized the Republicans, who were the majority party. The enfranchisement of the Negro was necessary to that party's control of the country and, as at Washington, must not be complicated by the question of suffrage for women. Both amendments lost, the defeat of that for Negro suffrage being of course blamed on the intrusion of the woman suffrage question.

Mr. Train performed one great service for the cause. During the Kansas campaign, he announced upon the platform, without consultation with any of the leaders, that when the campaign was over there would be a woman suffrage paper with Miss Anthony as manager, Mrs. Stanton and Parker Pillsbury as editors. Taken utterly by surprise there was nothing to do but accept this plan. The paper was to be called *Revolution*. Its motto was "Men, their rights and nothing more, women, their rights and nothing less." It was hampered by the necessity of printing Mr. Train's articles on extraneous matters, but the brilliant editorials of Mrs. Stanton and others gave it during its three years a nationwide hearing. As Mrs. Stanton said, "Some denounced it, some ridiculed it; but all read it." In its continuous campaign against the 15th Amendment it printed, to the discomfort of the Republicans, Lincoln's letter of 1836 in which he said, "I go for admitting all whites to the right of suffrage who pay taxes or bear arms, by no means excluding females," and with brilliant sarcasm it pointed out the bad logic and inconsistency of the party in departing from this stand of their great leader. Mr. Train and Mr. David M. Mellis were the financial backers, but the backing failed toward the end and left Miss Anthony with a debt of $10,000, which she herself paid through earnings from her speeches.

In 1870 Lucy Stone raised a fund of $10,000 to start the second suffrage paper, the *Woman's Journal*. Later she put a legacy of $10,000 into the paper. For the first two years Mary A. Livermore was the editor. After that Lucy Stone and her husband and later their daughter, Alice Stone Blackwell, issued it without fail each month till it was taken over by the Leslie Woman Suffrage Commission and became the *Woman Citizen* forty-five years later. For the most part the editorial labor and the financial burden were carried by these three people. Pioneers in the field of propagandist journalism, Mrs. Catt wrote of them, "They built up an enterprise compact of ideals, faith, and an endless generosity. Suffrage journalism has never been, could never be a business to this historic family of suffrage journalists. It has been a duty, a joy, a consecration, and an expense. . . . The suffrage success of today is not conceivable without the *Woman's Journal's* part in it."

The 14th Amendment was adopted in 1868, the 15th in 1870. For the first time the federal government assumed the right to dictate to the states the terms on which suffrage was to be granted to citizens and specifically stated that it was to be granted only to male citizens. Then began the long campaign described with such stirring eloquence by Mrs. Catt. "To get that word 'male' out of the Constitution cost the women of the country fifty-two years of pauseless campaign. Fifty-six campaigns of state referenda; four hundred and eighty campaigns to get legislatures to submit suffrage amendments; forty-seven campaigns to get constitutional conventions to write woman suffrage into state constitutions; two hundred and seventy-seven campaigns to get state party conventions and thirty campaigns to get presidential party conventions to include woman suffrage in party platforms; nineteen campaigns with nineteen successive Congresses and the final work of ratification. Millions of dollars were raised, mostly in small sums, and spent with economic care. Hundreds of women gave the accumulated possibilities of an entire life-time. Thousands gave years of their lives; hundreds of thousands constant interest and such aid as they could. It was a continuous, seemingly endless chain of activity. Young suffragists who helped forge the last links of that chain were not born when it began. Old suffragists who helped forge the first links were dead when it ended."

It was a campaign that for persistence and resourcefulness never has been equalled, and the arguments presented, if advanced on behalf of any other cause, would have won long before. One hardly knows which to marvel at the most,—the persistence of the women, the splendid support given by many men, or the astonishingly intricate mental processes of some of the gentlemen opposed. Consider a gem like this:

"Woman's true sphere is not restricted, but is boundless in resources and consequences. From the rude contact of life man is her shield. He is her guardian from its conflicts. He is the defender of her rights in his home, and the avenger of her wrongs everywhere.

"Married women being thus sheltered need nothing more from the state. The exceptional cases of unmarried females are too rare to change the general policy, while expectancy and hope constantly being realized in marriage are happily extinguishing the exceptions and bringing all within the rule that governs the wife and the matron."

The wage scale prevalent in 1865 shows that the theory of masculine protection did not extend to wage earners. Certain improvements were being made in the economic and social status of women and their educational opportunities were widening, but in New York they were making shirts at seventy-five cents a dozen. Domestics in Boston got from $1.50 to $3 a week. Woburn kept its women at work from eleven to thirteen hours and paid them two-thirds the wages of men. The highest wages quoted for women were in a glass factory, $4 to $8 a week. Women's wages were generally from one-half to one-third that of men. In the Kansas campaign one outraged legislator thundered that "of all the infernal humbugs of this humbugging woman's rights question the most absurd is that women should assume to be entitled to the same wages for the same amount of labor performed as a man."

In 1871 Miss Anthony, ever resourceful, attacked the problem posed by the recent amendments from a new angle. The attorney general of Nebraska had ruled that women were voters under the 14th Amendment. Many eminent lawyers and men in Congress agreed with him that the vote was included among the "privileges and immunities" which the amendment forbade any state to abridge. Miss Anthony therefore advised the women to test the question and about 150 in ten states and the District of Columbia did so. When the right to register and vote was denied action was brought against the inspectors and many able lawyers volunteered to conduct the cases.

In November, 1872 Miss Anthony and thirteen other women did vote in one ward in Rochester, New York. A few days later they were arrested, not by state police but by a United States marshal, on a criminal charge of having voted without a lawful right to vote. Mrs. Catt's comment on this unusual proceeding was that "authority for the United States government to take charge of the alleged violation of state election laws was laboriously drawn from the so-called Kuklux Klan law, which had been passed by Congress to prevent disfranchised rebels from exercising the right of suffrage before being pardoned." At the trial of Miss Anthony the judge directed the jury to bring in a verdict of guilty. When her counsel protested he not only refused to have the jury polled, but discharged it and fined her $100 and costs. On her refusal to pay the judge said the court would not order her committed and the matter rested there. The three inspectors who had allowed the women to vote were convicted and thrown into jail for not paying their fines. President Grant promptly remitted the sentence, and the men were so well fed and cared for by the suffragists during their week's imprisonment that Rochester got a great deal of fun out of the whole proceeding.

Chapter V

Wyoming: The First Surrender
adapted from
Woman Suffrage and Politics
Carrie Chapman Catt and Nettie Rogers Shuler

Chapter V

Wyoming: The First Surrender

After the start of the organized woman's rights campaign, in 1848, there were numerous conventions, meetings organized, speakers trained, and lists of friendly sympathizers made. Sooner or later somewhere a surrender of the age-old prejudice which had bound women to tutelage for many centuries would come. It happened in Wyoming.

The map of the United States, as represented in the geographies used in the public schools of the day, denoted most of the territory lying between Nebraska and the Rockies as the Great American Desert. Out of this vastness the federal government had carved a section large enough to accommodate an empire and called it Wyoming. A sparse and shifting population of adventurous men, sometimes with families, was scattered along the trails which led from Council Bluffs to Oregon or California. The Union Pacific Railroad was completed half-way across Wyoming in 1867 and a city of tents sprang up as if by magic at the last stop, called Cheyenne. Thousands of men poured in where dozens had been before—trappers, hunters, miners, all seekers of adventure.

The better class petitioned the Congress for the protection of an organized government. It was speedily granted, providing for a territorial government. The Territory was organized in May, 1869. The first election was to take place in September, its purpose being the choice of delegates to the first legislature.

At this point, twenty of the most influential men in the community, including all the candidates of both parties, were invited to dinner at the "shack of Mrs. Esther Morris, who had followed her husband and three sons into the trackless West." She was a newcomer with a complete understanding of the Eastern political treatment of Negro and of woman suffrage. In her ears were still ringing the words of Susan B. Anthony, one of whose public lectures she had heard just before setting out upon her western journey. To her guests she now presented the woman's case with such clarity and persuasion that each candidate gave her his solemn pledge that if elected he would introduce and support a woman suffrage bill. The election resulted in the choice of Wm. H. Bright, Democrat, who was elected president of the council when the legislature met, October 1, 1869. Many years after, in order that justice should be done the memory of Mrs. Morris, Captain Nickerson, the Republican candidate defeated in 1869 but elected in 1871, wrote the story, giving entire credit to Mrs. Morris for the act of the territory, and filed his documentary evidence at the county seat of Sweetwater County.

The 15th Amendment had not yet been ratified, but the law granting the vote to Negroes in territories to be organized was in force. The Wyoming September election reflected the hostility to Negro suffrage common in the country and was conducted in a manner to be expected of a turbulent population but recently brought under the discipline of law. The candidates and their friends spent money freely and every liquor shop was thrown open. Peaceful people did not dare walk the streets in some of the towns during the latter part of the day and evening.

At South Pass City, some drunken fellows with large knives and loaded revolvers swaggered around the polls, and swore that no Negro should vote. When one man remarked quietly that he thought the Negroes had as good a right to vote as any of them had, he was immediately knocked down, jumped on, kicked and pounded without mercy and would have been killed had not his friends rushed into the brutal crowd and dragged him out, bloody and insensible. There were quite a number of colored men who wanted to vote, but did not dare approach the polls until the United States marshal himself at their head and with revolver in hand, escorted them through the crowd, saying he would shoot the first man that interfered with them. There was much quarreling and tumult, but the Negroes voted. This was only a sample of the day's doings and was characteristic of the election all over the territory. The result was that every Republican was defeated and every Democratic candidate elected.

Mr. Bright, the newly elected president of the Council, was described by those who knew him as "a man of much energy and good natural endowments but without much school education." His wife was reported to be a woman of unusual attainments. Mrs. Morris had completely converted them both to woman suffrage.

Arrived at Cheyenne, Mr. Bright set himself to the task of converting to woman suffrage the twenty-two men who composed the two houses of the legislature. He reminded his fellow members that the legislature was unanimously Democratic and that, should it vote suffrage to women, it would show the world that Democrats were more liberal than Republicans who confined their extensions of the vote to Negroes; and that, should the Republican Governor veto the bill, it would give the Democrats a decided advantage. With all he argued the justice of the cause and pointed out that such an act would advertise the territory as nothing else could. Meanwhile, men and women in different parts of the territory wrote their delegates, urging support of the bill. The council, the territorial senate, without discussion passed the measure by a vote of ayes 6, nays 2, absent 1. In the house, the bill found a determined opponent—Mr. Ben Sheeks. A lively and acrimonious debate followed, and many amendments designed to kill the bill were introduced and voted down, one being that the word "woman" be stricken out, and the words "all colored women and squaws" be substituted. The original bill named eighteen years as the qualified age of the woman voter. A proposal to substitute twenty-one for eighteen was the only change made, and thus amended the bill passed, the council concurring.

Several of those who had voted for the bill, smarting under the gibes of outsiders who looked upon suffrage for women as wholly ridiculous, soon regretted having done so. Friends and foes alike turned to John W. Campbell, the unmarried Republican governor, and pleaded with him, some to sign, some to veto the bill. His interviewers found him vacillating and doubtful as to his duty. The determining factor proved to be a memory rising in the background of his mind, and growing each hour more vivid and persistent. In that memory he saw himself and other young boys, nineteen years before, stealing into the back seats of the Second Baptist Church in Salem, Ohio, his birthplace. The attraction was a woman's rights convention. The convention was the first in the state and differed in one respect from others at that period. It was entirely officered by women and "not a man was allowed to sit on the platform, speak or vote." The women issued an "address to Ohio women," a "memorial to the State Constitutional Convention" about to sit, and passed twenty-two resolutions, "covering the whole range of woman's political, religious, civil and social rights." Although greetings of encouragement were received from many of the chief leaders of the movement, the convention speakers were all Ohio women. When it was over, the men who had been in attendance met together and "endorsed all the ladies had said and done."

An episode so remarkable had not failed to make its impression upon the boy, although in the intervening years no occasion had arisen to transform the impression into conviction. Now the boy, grown to manhood, heard the voices once more, listened again to the arguments and knew no answer to their appeal. With his mind made up, in the words of ex-Governor Hoyt, "he saw that it was a long deferred justice and so signed the bill as gladly as Abraham Lincoln wrote his name to the Proclamation of Emancipation of the slaves."

"Of course," continues Mr. Hoyt, "the women were astounded! If a whole troop of angels had come down with flaming swords for their vindication, they would not have been much more astonished than they were when that bill became a law and the women of Wyoming were thus clothed with the habiliments of citizenship."

The two years which intervened before the next legislative election were eventful ones to the woman's cause in the territory. Soon after the passage of the bill, Mrs. Esther Morris was surprised by an appointment as justice of the peace at South Pass City. Owing to the fact that the population was sparse and regular courts were not yet numerous, a justice of the peace was an important officer and frequently heard types of cases which in after years went to other courts. The rowdies of the place undertook to intimidate Mrs. Morris and thus force her resignation, and incidentally prove that women were unequal to the performance of political duties, but they retired humiliated and discomfited from the contest. Nearly forty cases were brought before her and so justly did she administer them that not one was appealed to a higher court.

At the first term of the district court held after the first legislature women as well as men were drawn for grand and petit jurors. The first mixed grand jury was in session three weeks, during which time bills were brought for consideration of several murder cases, cattle and horse stealing and illegal branding, all of the bills commencing, "We, good and lawful male and female jurors on oath do say." When Justice Howe addressed this jury he said, "You shall not be driven by sneers, jeers, and insults of a laughing crowd from the temple of justice as your sisters have been from some of the medical colleges of the land."

The news of these women jurors spread far and wide. "King William of Prussia sent a congratulatory cable to President Grant upon this evidence of progress, enlightenment and civil liberty in America."

While arousing much discussion and winning approval among the law-abiding, women jurors were less popular among other classes, as was evidenced in the second legislature. The legislature of 1871 contained a minority of Republicans. Nine days after the legislature convened, a bill

Elizabeth Cady Stanton

Elizabeth Cady Stanton

Born in Johnstown, N.Y., daughter of Judge Daniel Cady and Margaret Livingston Cady. Attended Johnstown Academy and Troy Female Seminary. From childhood longed for the liberty and advantages denied to her sex. Was discovered tearing out of her father's law books the laws discriminating against women. Married in 1840 Henry B. Stanton, prominent abolitionist, went with him to London where he was delegate to the World's Anti-Slavery Convention. Here she met Lucretia Mott, one of the American "female delegates" whose credentials were refused by the convention. Her friendship with Mrs. Mott confirmed Mrs. Stanton's rebellion against woman's inferior social status, and the two women went back to America vowed to start a woman's rights movement. Carrying out this purpose, they called the first woman's rights convention in Seneca Falls, N.Y., June 19-20, 1848, thus launching the American feminist movement.

For many years, Mrs. Stanton was the chief propagandist and spokesman of the movement to enfranchise women. She was president of the National Woman Suffrage Association from its beginning in 1869, and on its amalgamation with the American Woman Suffrage Association, she served as president, 1890-1891.

She spoke before the New York Legislature in behalf of rights for married women in 1854, and again in 1860 demanding that drunkenness be made ground for divorce. For years she addressed Congressional hearings asking the submission of a Federal Amendment enfranchising women. She edited "The Revolution" during its short career, published her Woman's Bible in "The Woman's Tribune" (1895), was co-author of the first three volumes of "The History of Woman Suffrage" (1880-1886), published her reminiscences, "Eighty Years and More," in 1898. She was a woman of wide interests and strong convictions and no hesitancy in defending them. She died in 1902, non-conformist to the last.

MARY GRAY PECK

to repeal woman suffrage was introduced. The leader of the opposition in 1869, Ben Sheeks, was the only man in either house who had been returned. He was elected speaker of the house and devoted his entire attention to the repeal. It passed by a strictly party vote but was promptly vetoed by Governor Campbell, Republican, who in his message said that "to repeal it at that time would advertise to the world that women in their use of enfranchisement had not justified the acts of the members of the previous session and that such an imputation would be false and untenable." The house passed the repeal over the Governor's veto by the required two-thirds vote, but it failed by one vote in the council. No effort was ever again made to repeal woman suffrage in Wyoming.

Eighteen years after, a constitutional convention met in September to frame a constitution preparatory to statehood. In the preceding June, a woman's convention had been called and a hundred of the most prominent women of the territory had attended it. The purpose of the convention had been carried out in the adoption of the following resolution: "Resolved, That we demand of the constitutional convention that woman suffrage be affirmed in the state constitution."

Not a single delegate in the constitutional convention opposed woman suffrage, but one delegate proposed that the question be submitted to the people separately from the constitution, as it was likely to prove difficult for the state to get into the Union with woman suffrage in the constitution. The proposal brought a staunch and unyielding protest and the woman suffrage clause was included in the constitution.

The Committee on Territories in the House of Representatives recommended the admission of Wyoming, but William M. Springer, Democrat, of Illinois brought in a minority report of twenty-three pages, twenty-one devoted to objections to the woman suffrage article.

The territory was Republican and would send two Republicans to the Senate. The battle fiercely waged against its admission as a state was therefore led and chiefly supported by Democrats, woman suffrage furnishing a convenient excuse for opposition. The ghosts of reconstruction came forth from their hiding places and stalked the aisles of the United States Senate and House once more, making their presence known whenever the bill came up during a period of six months. Lengthy speeches by representatives from Alabama, Arkansas, Delaware, Georgia, Tennessee, Missouri and Texas, vituperative and ignorantly hostile, marked the opposition. "Woman suffrage will result in unsexing womanhood." "It is a reform against nature." "Let her stay in the sphere to which God and the Bible have assigned her." "They are going to make men of women, and the correlative must take place that men become women." During the debate, when it seemed impossible that the Congress would consent to the admission of Wyoming with woman suffrage in its constitution, delegate James Carey telegraphed the Wyoming legislature then in session and asked advice. The answer came back: "We will remain out of the Union a hundred years rather than come in without woman suffrage." This staunch response stiffened the faith of the friends and won votes of Republicans who were not yet ready to approve of woman suffrage. The bill of admission passed the House March 28, 1890.

The procedure was repeated in the Senate, action being postponed several times. The effort to amend by striking out woman suffrage having failed there also, the bill of admission was passed on June 27.

In the Congress Republicans opposed to woman suffrage had held quite unitedly that the state should have the right to decide who should vote within it. The Democrats, always contending that suffrage was a matter for the consideration of states, now refused to accept the principle and demanded a federal veto on state action. The bill passed by a party vote, Republicans voting for admission and Democrats against.

From the year 1869, every governor, chief justice and many prominent citizens of Wyoming have given endorsements of the beneficence of woman suffrage. "Not one reputable person in the state said over his or her own signature that woman suffrage is other than an unimpeachable success in Wyoming." At one time suffragists in the east were dismayed because Boston papers carried an interview with a "Prominent Gentleman from Wyoming," who declared that all the beliefs of the opponents of woman suffrage had proved true in that state. A telegram to the Mayor of Cheyenne asking for particulars concerning this "prominent gentleman" brought back the quick response: "A horse thief convicted by jury half of whom were women."

For fifty years Wyoming served as the leaven which lightened the prejudices of the entire world. She pronounced false every prediction of anti-suffragists and gave so much evidence of positive good to the community arising from the votes of women that she became the direct cause of the establishment of woman suffrage in all the surrounding states. Amid the gibes and the jests, the ridicule and the ribaldry, Wyoming stood fast through the generations, until the nation acknowledged that she was right and stood with her.

Chapter VI

Campaigning State by State
Maud Wood Park

Chapter VI

Campaigning State by State

Baffled in their attempts to get help from the Congress, suffrage leaders in the 1870's began to realize that federal action was unlikely so long as women were without political power. The obvious way of gaining it was to get woman suffrage in enough states to make women voters important in national politics.

Suffrage associations saw to it that a federal amendment was presented, and hearings given, in every Congress from 1878 on; but for nearly half a century, their major efforts went into state work. Complete enfranchisement by state constitutional amendments was the aim, though some form of partial suffrage, which could be granted by the legislatures, was frequently sought.

State amendments were hard to get. Besides the inertia and prejudice which all large changes in the social structure have to face, personal selfishness, entrenched interests, and machine politics were increasingly against woman suffrage. For them it meant that men must cede away half their political control, and that individuals or groups profiting by the old system must take the risks of a doubled electorate. In reality women in the suffrage ranks were outsiders, trying to storm the political fortress with no weapon except the appeal of justice to men within. Only as enfranchised citizens could they enter the stronghold and open its gates to sister women still outside. Whenever there was a split in party ranks, or a new party sprang up, the path of the suffragists was a little smoother. But usually the women had to depend on their own activity and such help as they could get from fair minded men, among whom the husbands of many workers were notable, for in suffrage ranks the term "friend husband" had a real meaning.

Then, too, the amending process in state constitutions presented many difficulties. It required passage by both branches of the legislature, often by more than a majority vote, and after that a referendum to the voters. In several states, passage by two consecutive legislatures was necessary; and some had a provision that the referendum could be carried only by a majority of all votes cast at the election, rather than of the votes on the amendment itself. In the later years of the struggle, the possibility in some states of getting an amendment submitted by means of initiative petitions removed a few obstacles. But there was never an easy way.

Between 1869 and 1890 lay twenty years of constant effort and constant defeat. The six years following held a few gains; the next fourteen only defeats. Between 1909 and 1916 there were some successes but more failures. Forty-one state amendment campaigns during forty-five years; nine victories, thirty-two failures! What faith it must have taken to keep on!

Again and again in the 70's and 80's Susan B. Anthony, Lucy Stone, Henry Blackwell travelled up and down the campaign states, where, as Alice Blackwell says, "they and the other speakers ate all kinds of food, slept in every sort of bed, were bitten by every variety of insect, faced all weathers, as well as storms of opposition, and were exposed to all the hardships of primitive conditions and pioneer life."

No victory during that period rewarded their sacrifices. Even two gains of territorial suffrage for women were snatched away: in Utah by action of the Congress, under the mistaken theory of reducing the percentage of Mormon vote; in Washington, by court decisions after two successive grants by the territorial legislature.

Many campaigns showed signs of bribery and election frauds. In Nebraska, in 1882, the women believed that fraudulent ballots had been used to defeat them. Michigan suffragists in 1912 were confident that their amendment carried, but was counted out. The well known legislative trick of "passing the buck" from one branch of the legislature to the other was frequently employed. The brewing and liquor interests, always active against woman suffrage, were particularly virulent in Ohio, Iowa, and Wisconsin. In some states where aliens were permitted to vote after a mere declaration of intention to become citizens, they were organized in blocks to defeat the amendment. At the first of five campaigns in South Dakota, Miss Anthony, then seventy years old, found blanketed Indians in the Republican convention, and when she addressed the Democrats, she was faced by a group of illiterate Russians, wearing large badges which said, "Vote against woman suffrage and Susan B. Anthony."

Only in partial suffrage was there any permanent advance between 1869 and 1890. The first step of that kind had been taken as far back as 1838, when Kentucky gave school suffrage to widows with children of school age. In 1861 Kansas had gone a little further by giving school suffrage to all women. In the 70's and 80's similar grants were made by fifteen states; and New Hampshire, Massachusetts and Montana gave to taxpaying women the right to vote upon questions submitted to the taxpayers. Then in 1887, Kansas granted municipal suffrage to its women.

Although our speakers liked to enumerate these scraps of suffrage as signs of progress, they often proved a handicap rather than an advantage. In Massachusetts the fact that only a small minority of eligible women usually voted in school elections was used at legislative hearings, year after year, by anti-suffragists seeking to prove that most women did not want to vote. In rebuttal, Alice Stone Blackwell, who always had necessary figures on the tip of her tongue, would point out that limited issues brought out a small vote where men were the only voters: but with committee members looking for an excuse to oppose a suffrage measure, her sound reasoning was of little avail. The election of an undesirable candidate when women had been among the voters, no matter how small their percentage, supplied a pretext for claiming that woman suffrage was harmful. In fact women voters, however few, made a convenient scapegoat when anything went wrong.

The year 1890, which saw the admission of Wyoming as a state, was marked also by the union of the two suffrage associations, the National and the American, into the National-American Woman Suffrage Association, with Elizabeth Cady Stanton as the first president and Lucy Stone as chairman of the executive committee. In spite of its double-barrelled name, which few persons outside its own membership ever mastered, the Association grew rapidly in strength and power.

Its early years were sunny ones. With the help of the Populist movement, Colorado, the first state to enfranchise women by a constitutional amendment, granted full suffrage in 1893. Idaho adopted a similar amendment, in 1896, and that same year suffrage was restored in Utah by the constitution under which the territory became a state.

For a long while those three contiguous states and their neighbor, Wyoming, made the only white spot on the suffrage map. They were pointed to with pride by suffragists, with contumely by opponents. The suffragists said: "Those four states are neighbors. If woman suffrage had been a failure in Wyoming, Colorado voters would surely have known about it and would have refused to enfranchise their own women. And if suffrage had not succeeded in the first two states, Idaho would never have tried it." In the dark years when there were no other gains, we wondered sometimes why the antis failed to retort, "Then why doesn't it keep on spreading?" But apparently none of them thought of that answer.

There were failures as well as victories even in the brief period of success, and after it came fourteen years of unbroken defeat in state amendment campaigns. Only a few scraps of partial suffrage and some changes for the better in the legal status of women gave any encouragement during those years.

Lucretia Mott, Lucy Stone and most of the other pioneers were dead by that time, and new leaders had come forward to shoulder the responsibility of the movement. Chief among them were Dr. Anna Howard Shaw and Mrs. Carrie Chapman Catt.

Dr. Shaw, vice-president of the Suffrage Association from 1891 to 1904 and then president until 1915, was, in the opinion of many critics, the foremost orator of her generation. Along with a golden voice, never raucous though easily heard in the largest halls, she had the gift of glowing and dramatic phrase, wit, humor, and an exaltation of appeal that swept audiences off their feet. Hers was the power to win hearts and sway opinions by the spoken word.

Mrs. Catt, who served for several years as chairman of the Association's organization committee, was chosen by Susan B. Anthony to succeed her as president, and served in that capacity from 1900 to 1904, and again from 1915 on. She brought to the closing years of the struggle tireless devotion, extraordinary executive ability, and breadth of vision such as only the greatest statesmen have possessed.

As a newcomer in the movement during the dark years at the beginning of the century, I was deeply stirred by the persistent courage of the women with whom I had the privilege of working. In Massachusetts at that time Alice Stone Blackwell and Mary Hutcheson Page, a woman with actual genius for raising money for the cause and enlisting valuable new workers, were trying to strengthen the state association, still suffering from the handicap of an unsuccessful test vote precipitated by opponents a few years earlier. Most of the newspapers were unfriendly. The Massachusetts Association Opposed to the Further Extension of Suffrage to Women—in order to save breath we usually referred to it as the M.A.O.F.E.S.W.—was determined in opposition. At the annual hearings on the "pestiferous perennial" the members of the legislative committee were visibly puffed up with pride over the anti assurances of complete confidence in the protection afforded by men.

In the summer of 1910, Mabel Willard and I went to a suffrage demonstration in London and found a spellbound crowd listening to Dr. Shaw, who was speaking from the parapet above the stone lions in Trafalgar Square. At dinner later, she told us that she had given up hope of another suffrage state during her lifetime. Yet she and thousands of others, who believed they were working only for future generations, never dreamed of letting up.

That very autumn their self sacrifice was rewarded by a victory. In Washington, after two previous defeats, a state suffrage amendment was carried. At last we had another state, a neighbor of the early four. The following year came California's successful campaign. No woman who gets her vote automatically when she is twenty-one will be likely to understand what that victory meant, for California was the first state with a considerable population to give votes to women.

For several days the result was in doubt. After the final news, late at night a reporter dashed up to the apartment of a suffrage worker. "I want to know what you think of the California victory," she called through the door. "Think! I'm standing on my head with joy," was the rash reply. For the next fortnight, our press clipping service was swamped with newspaper stories bearing the headline, "Boston Suffragist Stands on Her Head."

Eastern suffrage associations redoubled their efforts to help western campaigns. And help was needed, for the opposition, warned by the two recent successes, sharpened its attacks. On our side many new methods of work were tried: Open air meetings, where speakers talked from motor cars or soap boxes; processions; speeches at factory gates and between acts at theatres—anywhere and everywhere that we could get an audience.

Sometimes we stumbled on unexpected friends. We came across one in Ohio when we were helping local workers in a northern county during a referendum campaign. Old home week was being celebrated at the county seat and we drove over, in a decorated car, for the closing day. There we found that a circus was to have a tight-rope performance, preceded by a band concert, in the square late that afternoon. Letting no opportunity slip by, we asked the manager for permission to speak to the crowd between the concert and the acrobatic feat. He proved to be an Australian, enthusiastic about woman suffrage in his own country, and volunteered to introduce me. When the time came, he did so with as much gusto as if I had been a lady with two heads. Afterwards he invited us to join the circus procession back to the big tent and offered to let me speak from one of the rings during the regular performance. So our car fell in behind the elephants. Again I was introduced with flourishes. Unfortunately, a troupe of trained dogs, waiting for their turn, took offense at my voice and their yapping, combined with the noise of an engine on a nearby railway track, drowned my words. "Never mind," said the sympathetic manager, "if you'll let me get the pile of leaflets I saw in your car, I'll have them distributed," and in a few minutes the two clowns were giving our suffrage leaflets to the audience.

In 1912, suffrage amendments were submitted in six states and carried in Oregon, Arizona and Kansas. We were specially happy over Oregon, where the workers had faced five defeats.

Then, in 1913, the first territorial legislature of Alaska, by the first bill introduced, enfranchised the women of the territory; and Illinois opened the new path of presidential suffrage for women.

In the following year two of the seven state amendment campaigns were successful. Then in 1915, amendments were defeated in New Jersey, Pennsylvania, New York and Massachusetts. But within twenty-four hours, new campaigns were under way in all four.

Hard as the state by state road was, it led by 1916 to full suffrage for women in eleven states west of the Mississippi. With Illinois' presidential suffrage added, there were ninety-one members of the electoral college for whom women were entitled to vote. No longer were they a negligible factor in national politics.

Chapter VII
The Opposition Breaks
Gertrude Foster Brown

Chapter VII

The Opposition Breaks

The story of the winning of the vote by the women of Illinois, 1913, should bring a thrill to every woman of that state. That a group of inexperienced women, knowing nothing of the game of politics as played by men, in a state which contains the second largest city in the country with a long history of political corruption, should have been able to worst the most astute and intrenched political bosses, using only quiet, legitimate weapons, is something that history should not forget.

It began with a brilliant idea, quickly adopted and resolutely carried out. For more than twenty years the Illinois women had gone to the legislature asking for an amendment to the state constitution giving them the vote. At first only a handful, their number had grown so large that the legislature dreaded the frequent descent of trainloads of women. At every session the men braced themselves against the familiar assault, and breathed sighs of relief when it was over. They had no intention of giving in, but they were getting tired and temperish. So were the women. They knew that even if they won the legislative fight it would be only the beginning of a long and tiresome campaign—the question would have to be submitted to the voters, and they would have to convert a majority of the conservative and inert citizens of the state and persuade them to vote for the amendment. Then, even if they won, they might find themselves tricked and defrauded by the political bosses.

Under the Illinois law only one constitutional amendment could be passed at any one session of the legislature, and in working for a suffrage amendment the women alienated not only the reactionaries, but valuable friends who had amendments of their own they wished to have passed.

When Mrs. Grace Wilbur Trout was elected president of the state suffragists, with fine political sense she proposed that the women should drop their amendment and concentrate on asking the legislature for only so much suffrage as it had the right to bestow. This included not only the vote for many state and local offices—for all elective offices where the state constitution did not specify the word "male"—but also the vote for presidential electors.

The idea was not a new one. For years the national association had had a committee on presidential suffrage, and Illinois suffragists had had bills for both municipal and presidential suffrage in the legislature before. But it remained for Illinois women to demonstrate the value of the vote for president as a political weapon. Not only were they spared the long, difficult referendum campaign, but presidential suffrage proved to give women almost as great an influence on the Congress and the political parties as full suffrage. This plan, adopted by Mrs. Catt after she became president of the National American Suffrage Association, was a tremendous factor in the final victory.

The proposal was adopted with enthusiasm. Mrs. Catharine Waugh McCullough, an experienced Chicago lawyer, for many years chairman of the legislative committee of the state suffrage association, drew up the bill, and a new legislative chairman was chosen, a woman who had never been in Springfield, but who had made a notable record as a local leader.

Mrs. Sherman Booth was in a sanitorium when the news came to her that she was to direct the new state legislative campaign. At first it seemed to her preposterous. She had never seen the legislature in her life, she knew nothing about politics and less about politicians. However she believed firmly in woman suffrage, her husband believed in it as ardently, and both were willing to sacrifice for it. Finally Mrs. Booth agreed to undertake the task if she were given a free hand.

As soon as the November elections were over she sent for the Illinois Blue Book and began a study of the men who had been elected to the legislature. She cut out their pictures and started a card catalogue. On one side she pasted the picture. On the other she entered the man's name, his address and telephone number; his business, his church and club affiliations; his party and political district, his political boss and other influences effective with him; his own stand and that of his wife on suffrage; names of suffragists in his district; his record on public questions such as wet or dry, with space for remarks.

When the legislators went to Springfield for the opening of the session Mrs. Booth went with them, unknown and unremarked. For four weeks after the legislature opened the house was in a deadlock over who should be speaker.

Mrs. Booth sat in the house gallery studying the men on the floor, listening to the roll calls, learning all she could about each individual. By the end of the four weeks she had a pretty good knowledge of the legislators. She knew them all by face and name. She knew their records, and what they were interested in. She knew what could be expected from each. Her card catalogue had been checked over and corrected. About fifty of the legislators were known to be staunch friends of suffrage. Nearly as many more were bitter enemies whom it was hopeless to try to convert. This left about fifty men who might be persuaded to make up the necessary majority for suffrage.

The senate had passed a suffrage bill several times before only to have it go down in the house. No one was surprised, therefore, when, on May 7th, this bill slipped through the senate without a ripple. Every one knew that the house would kill it.

Illinois legislators usually go home for week-ends and come back to Springfield on a particular train on Sunday night. All the weeks of the session Mrs. Booth rode on this train. The journey offered an admirable chance to become friendly with one man after another. In a quiet way she became very popular. She was so pleasant, so unobtrusive, that men were not afraid of her. They liked to talk with her. She made a point of studying every man's hobby and encouraging him to talk about it. If a man were interested in registered pigs she knew something about registered pigs and was eager to learn more. She was so harmless and so winsome that as a man's acquaintance with her grew he became eager to help her. She became known as a friendly little woman whom many men would go out of their way to aid. She was so obviously helpless that even the bitterest antis did not worry about her.

Meanwhile Mrs. Trout had been working within the organization. She travelled everywhere over that big state, arousing the women, reviving their belief in the good the vote would do, stirring up their enthusiasm, until the entire organization was on the alert, ready to back up the Springfield leaders, whenever called on, in any way which might be demanded of them. Where Mrs. Booth was ready with quiet, logical arguments, Mrs. Trout was eloquent, persuasive, full of touching stories. Her pleas, earnest and full of emotion, converted certain men whom Mrs. Booth could not win. Another kind of help was given by Ruth Hanna McCormick, the daughter of Mark Hanna, who had inherited much of her father's political ability. Medill McCormick was a member of the legislature and both he and his wife were ardent suffragists. Mrs. McCormick was particularly effective with the press. She took the regular newspaper correspondents in Springfield into her confidence and made them valuable allies. They withheld or sent out suffrage news as it would best help the campaign.

One of the most powerful men in the legislature was also one of the most hostile to suffrage. He represented the Democratic wets of Chicago. It was said that he rarely made a promise, but that when he once gave his word he could be relied on to keep it. Mrs. Booth went to him and asked for fair play.

"I know you are opposed to suffrage," she said, "but won't you help us get the bill in the hands of a good committee, and on the calendar so it will at least be voted on?"

"What are your chances?" he asked.

"If I tell you will you use it against us? I know you have the power to keep the bill from passing, but they say we can trust your word. If I give you the facts will you use them to hurt us?"

"No, I won't," he said.

So she told him frankly how things stood, and he agreed to bring up the bill when she was ready, and let her have a vote on it.

"Let me know from time to time how you are getting on," he added.

She continued her quiet campaign of persuasion, backed more and more effectively by the suffragists of the state. At just the right moment a man would hear from his constituents in a way he could not ignore. Letters and telegrams and week-end conversations with his best friends, every channel by which he could be reached was enlisted to win him over. And one by one the men gave in. One after another they promised to vote, not always for the suffrage bill but to vote down amendments which would nullify it, so that at least it would not be killed without a vote. "Give us fair play," was all the women asked. "We want a vote on our measure. We suppose we'll be beaten, but at least give us a chance."

From time to time Mrs. Booth went to her friendly enemy and reported progress. "So and so has been won over," she would say.

"Did he say he would vote for your bill?" he would ask.

"Yes."

"Have you got it in writing?"

"No."

"Then don't count on him," or "You can trust his word," he would advise.

More votes were needed, especially among the Democrats, and Mrs. Antoinette Funk came down from Chicago. Mrs. Funk was a practising lawyer, attractive, impetuous, eloquent and persuasive and a good Democrat. It was not long before she had some of the most hostile Democrats won, not to vote for the bill, but not to fight it.

At length it was reported out of committee. It passed its first reading without creating much attention, then it came to a second reading and surprised the house by having an impressive majority against every attacking amendment. One of the most vitriolic enemies of woman suffrage, a man whose scathing opposition was most feared, sat silent because of his friendship for Mrs. Funk. Until now there had been little talk about the measure. The work had been so quietly done that few realized how much progress the women had made. Man after man had stipulated, in promising his vote, "don't tell any one," and the women were only too glad to keep faith with him. No one but they themselves and their friendly enemy knew how strong they were. The opposition were baffled. With all their influence they could not find out what the suffrage chances really were. Anton Cermak, head of the United Liquor Dealers Association, came down to direct the fight against what seemed to have developed into a real menace.

The speaker was a new man, young and inexperienced. He had promised the women to let them have their chance, but opponents brought such an array of powerful influences to bear that he was wavering. After the second reading, to gain time the opposition persuaded him to put off the third and final reading. The legislators were eager to get home for the week-end, and they adjourned, leaving the matter in mid-air. The unwarranted delay aroused the women all over the state. Many times with great difficulty, they had been prevented from descending on Springfield. Now they wanted to come, en masse, to force action. "Don't let them come," advised friendly members of the legislature. "You'll never be able to hold your men if a crowd of women come down here."

The young speaker, haggard and worn from the conflicting pressure, appealed to Mrs. Trout for further evidence of suffrage strength. During his week-end the women brought all their forces into action. They made the wires hum. His telephone rang constantly with appeals for his support, and on Monday morning, when he returned to Springfield, he found his desk massed high with letters and telegrams. As Mrs. Booth followed him in, she asked, "Do you still think any one in the state is opposed to suffrage?" and he threw up his hands.

That morning the opposition used every possible tactic to prevent the bill from coming to its final vote. The women were ready. The card index was complete. Every man had been checked over and over. There were seven more votes promised for suffrage than the required majority. Messages had been sent to every friend of the measure urging him not to fail to be present for the vote. On the floor of the house itself were "captains," each a friendly member in charge of a certain number of men. In the gallery sat Mrs. Booth and Mrs. McCormick with the list of members, and Mrs. Trout stood guard at the entrance to the floor of the house to see that no friendly member left his seat, and to prevent any unfriendly lobbyist from violating the law by entering after the session opened. Mrs. Funk acted as messenger between the floor and the gallery. Attempts were made to get Mrs. Trout to leave her post. She was even threatened with arrest. But she knew the law, and for that

Susan B. Anthony

Susan B. Anthony

The life of Susan B. Anthony is an amazing story of nearly sixty years of devotion, singleness of purpose and unbelievable persistence for the enfranchisement of women. Her Quaker inheritance and early training aroused in her a spirit of resentment against the injustices in a man-ruled world.

She was organizer and director of countless activities, attended hearings and conducted campaigns, of which she was ever the driving force. She issued the call to conventions and guided and directed their activities. She worked in every capacity and did not consent to become president of the National American Woman Suffrage Association until 1892, serving till her eightieth birthday, in 1900. She remained honorary president until her death.

The Cause suffered defeat after defeat and yet she never lost sight of the main objective—an amendment to the Constitution of the United States enfranchising women. Through hatred, persecution and bitter disappointment she struggled on, finally to be accorded recognition, admiration, honor and affection, even by those who opposed her cause.

She said: "Cautious, careful people, always casting about to preserve their reputation and social standing, never can bring about a reform. Those who are really in earnest must be willing to be anything or nothing in the world's estimation and publicly and privately, in season and out, avow their sympathy with despised ideas, and their advocates, and bear the consequences," and again "If I have made a success of my life, the one great element in it has been 'constancy of purpose'—not allowing myself to be switched off the main road, or tempted into by-paths of other movements."

The story of her life is an inspiration in a world filled with lost causes.

EMMA B. SWEET
Cousin and Secretary of Miss Anthony

one day no one went on to the floor of the house who was not entitled to.

The tension in the chamber could be felt. Newspaper men were on the *qui vive*. They knew that a big story was about to break. The wets were more than uneasy. They could not find out what the situation was, but they were afraid, and all morning long they delayed the vote, hoping that the house, tired and hungry, would adjourn for luncheon. They brought up one point of order after another. They demanded a roll call on each one, and each showed the suffrage strength. But still the vote was delayed.

Mrs. Booth sent her friendly enemy a note "Please, please don't let them adjourn without a vote." Noon passed, one o'clock, two o'clock, and still the opposition was strong enough to prevent the vote being taken. Finally, after three o'clock, the third reading was called.

The voting began in the midst of a tense silence. As man after man responded to the call the two women watching in the gallery checked off the ayes. The end of the first roll call came and suffrage had not polled enough votes to win. On the second roll call, still suffrage had not carried.

By this time the excitement was so intense that both men and women were weeping. Only Mrs. Booth was calm. From the gallery she sought the eyes of her friend on the floor below and she dropped him a piece of paper. It contained the names of seven men whose votes had not yet been recorded.

"Please see that these men vote," she begged. It was only a few minutes before the men were found, but the strain seemed almost more than could be borne.

"Ayes 83, noes 58" declared the Speaker, and pandemonium broke loose.

But the battle was not yet over. It was one of the hottest summers that that hot Illinois town has ever known, but Mrs. Booth stayed on in Springfield. When the bill came from the engrossing clerk there were strange mistakes in it, which would have caused it to be thrown out as defective. These were corrected. Then every pressure was brought to bear on the governor to prevent him from signing the measure, and he delayed long enough to cause considerable anxiety. Finally the constitutionality of the law was attacked. A case was brought against the Chicago election commissioners for allowing women to vote on a local question. The local courts gave a favorable decision, but the opposition engaged the ablest lawyers in the state and carried the case to the Illinois Supreme Court.

Counsel equally powerful must be secured to plead the suffrage case but the women had no money. The campaign had cost only $1567, printing, stenographic help, telegrams, hotel bills and everything; but the suffrage treasury was empty. In this emergency, the *Chicago Examiner,* owned by William R. Hearst, offered to let the women bring out a special edition of the paper and to give them the entire proceeds, Mr. Hearst himself assuming the costs. It meant six more weeks of the hardest work during that hot summer, but with this generous help the suffragists made such a brilliant success of the edition that they cleared $15,000 and thus were able to secure adequate counsel for their case.

The decision of the Supreme Court was long delayed. Meanwhile the women worked at top speed to bring out a big registration of women for the municipal election in the spring of 1914. The opposition had prophesied that less than 25,000 would register but 200,000 registered in Chicago alone.

Somewhat later the General Federation of Women's Clubs held its biennial convention in Chicago, and for the first time a resolution endorsing woman suffrage was to be introduced on the floor of the convention.

The Federation had always been unwilling to introduce controversial questions and so far suffrage had come under that head. Two years before, in San Francisco, the convention had refused to allow a similar resolution to be presented. Still there were many ardent suffragists in the Federation and, if the question were permitted to come to a vote, it was believed it was sure to pass. The new president, Mrs. Percy A. V. Pennybaker of Texas, was a suffragist, she was also a magnetic speaker and a master parliamentarian. Through her skillful management the resolution was presented just as the suffragists wanted it, and so great had been the change in sentiment in the two years that it carried almost unanimously.

That evening a banquet was given by the Illinois Suffrage Association to the clubwomen of the Federation. Enthusiasm ran high over this action by the largest body of women in the country, and when it became known that the Supreme Court had that day confirmed the right of the Illinois women to the presidential and partial vote, the excitement was boundless. Messages of congratulation poured in from all over the country, as well they might, for this was the most important victory suffrage had ever won. It meant for the first time a break in the solid mass of antisuffrage states east of the Mississippi River, and now the votes of twenty-nine congressmen from Illinois were added to the suffrage sentiment in Congress.

As I sat with Mrs. Booth and her husband some years ago and they told me the tale of the winning of Illinois, he, strangely enough, remembering better than she the details of the long struggle, it was the listening young people who marked for us how far the world has moved since then. Their son and daughter, then grown, sat round-eyed and enthralled by the story. They had never heard it. Did women, just because they were women, ever have to fight against such incredible odds? And was it their mother who had played the leading role on such a stage? Like most young people they had always taken her for granted—retiring, thoughtful, quiet and kind, just a mighty nice mother—and suddenly they saw her a general, a heroine in one of the great dramas of the world. For this Illinois victory was the turning point in the enfranchisement of twenty-five millions of women.

Chapter VIII

Appeals to Congress
Penelope P. B. Huse

Chapter VIII

Appeals to Congress

Efforts for federal action in favor of woman suffrage had not been confined to petitions of remonstrance during the years of discussion on the 14th and 15th Amendments. In 1866 a bill to enfranchise the citizens of the District of Columbia gave an opportunity to include women in its provisions. Senator Anthony of Rhode Island made a notable speech in its favor. It was defeated after floods of oratory had been poured out and all the arguments against woman suffrage used, that, taken out of moth balls, dusted and refurbished, were to serve in every debate in the coming fifty-three years.

When it was evident that the 14th Amendment was to pass, though nothing could move such once staunch supporters of equal rights as Gerrit Smith and Wendell Phillips to protest against its injustice, a handful of faithful friends in the Congress made a counter attack. In 1868 Senator Pomeroy of Kansas and Representative Julian of Indiana introduced resolutions that the basis of suffrage should be citizenship and that all native or naturalized citizens should enjoy this right equally. The Julian resolution added "without distinction founded on sex."

The American Equal Rights Association, the name adopted at the convention of 1866, made this resolution its special object. It also backed the resolution passed at its convention in St. Louis in 1869, which held that under the

Constitution women were citizens, entitled under the 14th Amendment to all the privileges of citizenship, including suffrage. Copies of both resolutions were sent to every member of Congress. Mrs. Stanton appeared at a hearing before the congressional committee on the District of Columbia bill in 1870. In this year also Victoria Woodhull's memorial was presented to Congress and given a hearing before the Judiciary Committee of the House. In 1872 Mrs. Stanton and others appeared at a hearing before the Judiciary Committee of the Senate asking consideration of a "declaratory act" which would protect women in the right of suffrage should they exercise it under the 14th Amendment.

Extraordinary resentment of these efforts was shown by the Republican press. Possibly through a sense of guilt because the party was deserting the women in this crisis when they had so loyally supported it, the papers resorted to cheap abuse. The signers of the petitions were described as having "hook-billed noses, crow's feet under sunken eyes, and a mellow tinting in the hair."

"Heaven forbid" cried one newspaper, "that we should think of any of the number as a married woman without a fervent aspiration of pity for the weaker vessel who officiates as her spouse. As to rearing children, that is not to be thought of in this connection. What iconoclast shall break our idol by putting the ballot in woman's hand?"

The New York *Tribune* pictured the petitioners as "languishing their lives away in a mournful singleness from which they can escape by no art in the construction of waterfalls or the employment of cotton padding," (large busts being fashion's order of the day). The *Tribune* went on that woman did not need the ballot "when she rules the world by a glance of the eye," and ended by stating that "the sure cure for such ills as the Massachusetts petitioners complain of is a wickerwork cradle and a dimple cheeked baby." This must have seemed slightly ironical to Mrs. Stanton, who had often been kept from work for suffrage because she had just had or was just going to have, another baby.

The Republican national platform of 1872 had however a "splinter" in favor of woman suffrage, the first that ever appeared in the platform of any great party.

> "The Republican party, mindful of its obligations to the loyal women of America expresses gratification that wider avenues of employment have opened to women, and it further declares that her demands for additional rights should be treated with respectful consideration."

This same year the women anti-suffragists began petitioning Congress to protect them from enfranchisement on the grounds that "Holy Scripture inculcates a different and for us a higher sphere apart from public life . . . that we find a full measure of cares, duties, responsibilities devolving upon us, and are therefore unwilling to bear other and heavier burdens and those unsuited to our physical organization . . . that an extension of suffrage would be adverse to the interests of the working women of the country . . . and because these changes would introduce a fruitful element of discord into the existing marriage relation, which would tend to the infinite detriment of children and increase the already alarming prevalence of divorce throughout the land."

In 1874 Senator Sargent of California offered an amendment to a bill creating a new territory, which would make women eligible to vote there. Though defeated nineteen senators voted for it, which was an encouraging gain. In 1876 a memorial was presented asking establishment of a government in the District of Columbia which should include women as voters, but no action resulted. In the meantime the Supreme Court had decided in the case of Mrs. Minor of St. Louis, that she was not entitled to vote under the 14th Amendment. The National Suffrage Association therefore began again its demand for the "16th Amendment," but it was not until 1878 that Senator Sargent introduced by unanimous consent the joint resolution that forty-two years later became the 19th Amendment. It read:

> "The right of the citizens of the United States to vote shall not be abridged by the United States or by any state on account of sex. Congress shall have power to enforce this article by appropriate legislation."

At long last the issue was drawn, clear cut. Hearings were granted and petitions signed by 30,000 women were submitted. For two days eminent men and women presented their views. The committee brought in an adverse report, which explained blandly that women suffered no disabilities before the law; that all these had been swept away; that the courts and juries favored women over men; that their appeals to legislatures against injustice never went unheeded; and that as any state could grant suffrage to women and some had, "with perhaps good results" it was "unwise and inexpedient to enable three-fourths of the states . . . to force woman suffrage on the other fourth in which the public opinion of both sexes might be strongly averse to such a change."

Senator Hoar of Massachusetts as member of the Committee on Privileges and Elections before which the resolution had lain, presented a masterly minority report, signed also by Senator Mitchell of Oregon and Senator Cameron of Pennsylvania. Oddly enough a week after this a bill allowing women to practice before the Supreme Court was signed by President Hayes.

The appointment of special committees in both Senate and House to consider "memorials, petitions, bills and resolutions asking for extension of suffrage to women" was a step forward, although the House committee did not long survive. The 16th Amendment was reported favorably by the Senate committee in 1882, 1884, 1886, 1889, and 1893 and later. The first vote in the Senate on the Amendment was taken on January 25th, 1887 with 16 yeas, 34 nays and 26 absent. No other vote was taken in the Senate until 1914 or in the House until 1915, although hearings were held constantly, and in 1883 and 1890 the Judiciary Committee of the House reported favorably.

The two major political parties during all this long and trying period had made woman suffrage their football. The question was never considered rationally by the men in Congress but always emotionally if considered at all. To read the speeches delivered by these Solons at the hearings is enough to make reason totter on its throne. It was not unusual to have the same man argue first that women should not be enfranchised because if given the vote they would spend all their time on politics, leaving home, husband and children neglected; and second that they should not be enfranchised because they did not want the vote, would not use it and were not interested in politics.

In 1900 Susan B. Anthony, who had led the movement for so many years, retired as president of the national association and was succeeded by Carrie Chapman Catt. Possibly no woman in the country was more revered and respected for her character and her intellect than Miss Anthony, and the messages sent her on her retirement, coming from all over the world, were a remarkable tribute to her, both as a woman and as leader of a great cause.

Younger women were now coming into the movement. More states had been won and in 1912 the Senate Committee on Woman Suffrage was favorable, but the hearings before it and before the Judiciary Committee of the House were fruitless. In 1913, Dr. Anna Howard Shaw who had been president of the national association from 1904 appointed Alice Paul head of the long-standing congressional committee.

One of its first pieces of effective publicity was a well planned and impressive parade held in connection with the inaugural of President Wilson. About 8,000 women were in line and tremendous crowds had turned out to watch the elaborate spectacle, with its floats, banners and beautiful costumes. Hoodlums were allowed by the police to break through the procession, slap, trip up, spit upon and insult the marching women. Some on floats were pulled off, others were knocked down, and one of the most disgraceful scenes ever enacted on the streets of the capital shocked those who watched while the police stood idly by. Soldiers from Fort Meyer were called to restore order. The episode resulted in a congressional investigation and the chief of police was dismissed. The indignation aroused and voiced by the press all over the country stirred new interest in the suffrage movement. The Senate committee reported the Amendment favorably and for the first time unanimously. There was however no action by the House Judiciary Committee.

Energetic as had been the work of the congressional committee under Alice Paul, it developed that she was not only acting as head of this committee under appointment of Dr. Shaw, but that she had formed and was acting as leader of a separate organization called the Congressional Union, to work for the federal amendment independently of the National American Woman Suffrage Association. This meant duplication of effort by an organization over which the national association would have no control, and whose methods, borrowed from the English suffragists, were radically at variance with those of the national association. Miss Paul was asked to resign from the committee of the national association and Mrs. Medill McCormick was appointed in her place.

The Suffrage Amendment was called the 17th after the proclamation of the Income Tax Amendment in 1913 but after the passage of the 17th, that on the election of senators, no prophetic number was used. A new form of amendment sponsored by Senator Shafroth of Colorado was favorably reported in the Senate and the House in 1914. Its object was to increase the number of suffrage states and so serve as a support to the pending Amendment. The National American Woman Suffrage Association voted to support the old form and "such other legislation as the National Board may authorize and initiate, to the end that the long-standing Federal Amendment, introduced in 1872, shall become a law." This caused confusion however, and fortunately after a few months the Shafroth resolution was abandoned.

There was no action on the amendment in 1915 after the defeat in the House in January. Mrs. McCormick had resigned. Mrs. Frank Roessing had succeeded her and ceaseless activity went on. No one who has not taken part in congressional lobby work can have any idea of what it involves. It includes interviews with members of Congress preceded by innumerable fruitless attempts to make appointments; hours spent walking the corridors of the House and Senate office buildings trying to run to earth some man not too busy or too indifferent to see you; sitting in his office listening patiently and with good humor to arguments which you have had dished up by dozens of other Congressmen; to reasons which are unconvincing; to funny stories with no point; putting up with abuse and misunderstanding; bearing with long and boring reminiscences of female relatives who do not want the vote, or possibly do; trying to pin him down to a definite promise to vote for the amendment and leaving the office to go through all this again with the next man interviewed. Only those with a sense of humor can last long in this sort of duel.

Rereading the opposition's speeches of these fifty years, one is amazed that their inanities could ever have been taken seriously. With infinite patience, good humor and persistence, the women carried on one campaign after another, winning a point here and a point there. Only an abiding faith in the principle for which they fought could have inspired such selfless devotion to an unpopular cause.

Anna Howard Shaw

Anna Howard Shaw

Anna Howard Shaw, suffragist, minister, doctor of medicine and author, was born at New Castle-on-Tyne, February 14, 1847. Her family came to the United States in 1851, settling first in Massachusetts and later, on a wilderness claim in northern Michigan.

The spirit of her ancestors, the Stotts and the "fighting Shaws" of Castle Loch-an-Eilan, gave her courage for a tragic early life and helped her endure the rigid economy and loneliness of college and theological school. By 1885 she had served as pastor of two Massachusetts churches and taken a degree in medicine. Significant is the fact that on account of sex she was refused ordination by the New England Conference and the Methodist Episcopal church. In the same year the Methodist Protestant church ordained her.

Temperance, then suffrage roused her zeal for a righteous cause. Her success as organizer and speaker for suffrage led to the presidency of the National American Woman Suffrage Association in 1904. In 1915 she was chosen honorary president. While in office she raised the membership of the Association from 17,000 to 200,000.

When the United States entered the World War Dr. Shaw was called to the chairmanship of the Woman's Committee of the Council of National Defense, and later joined a distinguished group of speakers for the League of Nations Covenant. She passed at Moylan, Pennsylvania, July 2, 1919.

Candor, good judgment and a compassionate interest in her fellow men were secrets of Dr. Shaw's power. She was witty and frank and charmed with her gaiety and gallantry. She passed into history as the great suffrage orator, who as she advanced her cause became a living demonstration of the power of women and the moral force of a right idea.

JUSTINA L. WILSON

CHAPTER IX

A Decisive Victory Won
Gertrude Foster Brown

Chapter IX

A Decisive Victory Won

For more than sixty years New York had been at once the hope and the despair of suffragists. They were convinced that if New York could be won there would be enough suffrage representatives in Congress to force the suffrage amendment through. But New York was a staggering problem. Every year since the Civil War a suffrage bill had been presented to the legislature only to be killed in committee. Tammany Hall Democrats in the city and the Republican machine up-state, equally corrupt, waged never ending warfare against each other, but were a unit against woman suffrage.

But suffrage sentiment was growing. Under the inspiring leadership of Carrie Chapman Catt, suffragists had adopted a new form of organization which brought the full force of their numbers to bear on the political parties in a way they could not fail to understand.

Mrs. Catt, a westerner by birth, had had years of campaigning with Susan B. Anthony. Succeeding Miss Anthony as president of the National American Woman Suffrage Association, in 1900, with the warm sympathy and help of Mr. Catt, she had carried on the work tirelessly for four years when her health broke and she had retired. She was a handsome woman, gracious in manner, a logical and eloquent speaker. Coming back into the movement in 1909, after the death of her husband, with wise statesmanship she began to organize the women as the political parties were organized, by assembly and election districts. The first city convention of the newly organized Woman Suffrage Party packed Carnegie Hall and attracted great attention from both politicians and the press.

In 1912 the new Progressive Party at their New York state convention endorsed woman suffrage. The Republicans and Democrats could do no less. As a result, at the next session of the legislature the suffrage bill passed both houses, and suffragists were assured that it would be passed again by the legislature of 1915. This meant that the question would come before the voters at the election in November, 1915.

In England, as in Scandinavia, women had obtained the vote through a simple majority in parliament. In the United States, suffrage could only come through a constitutional amendment, federal or state. In New York State, an amendment to the constitution must be passed by two different and successive legislatures, and then submitted to the voters. At that time the Empire State had a population of about 9,000,000, of whom 2,700,000 were foreign born. New York women, therefore, were subject to an electorate containing a large proportion of men of other nationalities, some of whom could not read their ballots.

Now, with their amendment on its way through the legislature, the suffragists had less than two years to win over this heterogeneous mass of voters. The New York State Woman Suffrage Association was the oldest and largest of the suffrage organizations in the state. At its call most of the smaller ones combined their forces in the

Empire State Campaign Committee and persuaded Mrs. Catt to be their chairman.

The outlook was discouraging. Responses to a questionnaire sent to prominent suffragists showed that not one believed that her county could organize or finance even its own work. Few thought they could raise any money at all.

Nothing daunted, Mrs. Catt set to work to build a state wide Woman Suffrage Party along political lines. The key to the organization was the assembly district. The state was divided into twelve campaign districts and a leader appointed for each one. Under the campaign district leaders were the leaders in each of the assembly districts in that territory, and under each assembly district leader a captain was planned for each of the election districts, the polling precincts of which the assembly district was composed. For the first time suffragists had a political machine with which they could meet the politician on his own ground.

There were practically no experienced workers. Training schools were held in nearly every county in the state to find leaders, to train them in political organization, in campaign methods, and in money raising. Every leader faced long hard hours of work, begging of money, meeting problems of personality, paying her own expenses, with no political job in sight as reward—no return of any kind.

There were no radios and no effective talking pictures, at that time. The only way of reaching voters was through a personal appeal. It was useless to invite men to come to suffrage meetings. Where they were not opposed, they were indifferent, or considered the whole business a joke. Since they would not come to women, suffragists had to go to them wherever they were.

In the days of trailing skirts and picture hats to see a woman mount a soap box on a street corner, or stand on the back seat of an automobile, and begin to orate, was so startling that men could not help but stop and listen. The street meetings were so effective that soon, all over the state, women held their meetings on street corners or public squares, wherever traffic was heaviest, with gay banners and much literature. They haunted every place where men gathered. His clubs, his conventions, his amusement places, were never safe from the danger of a speech demanding votes for women. Vaudeville performances were staged by suffragists. They spoke between the acts in theatres.

The first parades were small and timid affairs. In May, 1911, 3,000 women and 89 men were in line. A year later, 10,000 women marched, and, in 1915, 40,000. Always in New York the women were received with respect. Not so the men sympathizers. Jeers and scurrilous remarks were showered on them. The mildest was "Go home and wash the dishes" or "Rock the baby."

The parades were striking evidence of the sweeping progress of the movement. Women from every class and walk in life, and from every kind of employment were in line. Women from luxurious homes, from the tenement districts, girls from the workshops of the lower East side, trade union women, teachers and professional women, young girls and elderly women—all united for a common cause.

Stunts were many and appealing. Block parties had street dancing for each foreign group in turn, with native costumes and music, and suffrage speeches in the native tongue. Irish banners with shamrock literature and suffrage speeches greeted workmen in the subway excavations. Banks and trust companies were "raided" by suffragists with speeches and literature. A White Wings' Day for street cleaners had tiny brooms as souvenirs. For a week car barns rang with oratory directed to the 240,000 men employed on the street cars. There was a Firemen's Day, a Barber's Day; and a Telephone and Telegraph Day gave excuse for asking prominent men their views on suffrage.

All this made good copy. The suffrage press department, headed by Rose Young, a clever and experienced writer, furnished the papers day to day with feature stories. Of the fifteen dailies in New York City, ten, including the *Tribune, World, Evening Post* and, in some measure, the *Evening Sun,* supported suffrage editorially. The *Times* though editorially opposed gave much space to suffrage news.

A press and publicity council, organized by Mrs. Norman de R. Whitehouse, composed of artists, writers and some well known society women, undertook the task of creating news and thus increasing publicity, and of seeing that antisuffrage articles and editorials were adequately answered.

They were full of new ideas—a boxing match for suffrage, the opening game of the Giants-Chicago Cubs sponsored by suffragists, a suffrage "Hopperie" at Coney Island. They had a Woman's Independence Day, like a Fourth of July celebration. In a more serious vein was the appearance in a naturalization court of a group of university women in their caps and gowns who sat in silent protest while thirty men, including Turks, Persians, Russians and Serbs, received their final papers—new citizens from whom American women had to beg the vote.

Masses of literature were provided by a special educational committee of which Mrs. Howard Mansfield was chairman. Small leaflets, "flyers," which told in the simplest language why women wanted the vote, and answered objections, were printed in such quantities that they cost only 22 cents a thousand, and the state was snowed under with them.

In working for the vote many women of means for the first time in their lives came in close touch with working girls. They learned of the long hours of work and the pitifully small wages of those days. They saw how much more quickly changes in laws for working women were made in states where they had the vote. Among the working girls were some remarkable leaders who not only organized in their own ranks, but who became popular speakers in drawing rooms. Led by Miss Mary A. Dreier, and Rose Schneiderman, they organized effective workers, especially among trade union men.

School teachers were another strong force for suffrage. Under Katherine Devereux Blake, 12,000 formed a teachers' section, and worked tirelessly for suffrage, giving their vacations without pay.

Mrs. Catt had insisted on having a campaign fund of $20,000 before she would undertake the chairmanship of the Empire State Campaign Committee, and this money she had to raise mostly herself. As a contrast, at the beginning of the second year of the campaign $105,619 was pledged at one mass meeting in Carnegie Hall.

The ideal set by Mrs. Catt, of reaching every voter with a personal appeal, was pursued doggedly. No one could count the thousands of miles covered by weary feet as women canvassed apartment and tenement houses, shops and factories, immense office buildings, making personal appeals and getting signatures to slips promising to vote for woman suffrage. Theoretically, an election district captain had only an average of 350 voters in her election district. With a committee of ten women in each election district, which was the goal set, each woman had only thirty-five men to canvass.

The climax of the campaign was the great banner parade, which veteran policemen said was the greatest street demonstration the city had ever seen, and which the headlines of New York newspapers called "a magnificent pageant—a spectacle never before equalled in this or any other country." It lasted from morning into the evening, and the rear was brought up by hundreds of motor cars, gay with Chinese lanterns. Long after darkness fell the avenue was a solid mass of moving colored lights. As a tired woman packed up her literature a burly policeman said, "Wha' cher working so hard fer? Ye've got the game won."

Indeed it almost seemed so. Enthusiasm in the state was running high. New York City under the direction of Mary Garrett Hay, one of the most expert of the leaders, had been organized and campaigned to the last outpost. While the rest of the state had been slower in getting into action all the large cities had adopted the Woman Suffrage Party plan. Every one knew that its success would be a miracle after so short a campaign, but the women could not but hope that the miracle was about to happen.

Suffragists had experienced so many fraudulent elections that early in the campaign, Harriot Stanton Blatch, wise daughter of Elizabeth Cady Stanton, obtained from the legislature a law permitting women to watch at the polls on election day. All through the year, at training schools, women were prepared for this work.

On November 2, before daybreak, in thousands of homes, women were dressed for their jobs, sandwiches were prepared, thermos bottles filled with hot coffee, enough not only for themselves but for the election officials. At six o'clock, when the polls opened, women watchers were at their posts inside the polling places. Outside were women pickets with "Votes for Women" posters, literature and sample ballots.

Instructions had been sent out by political headquarters to treat the suffragists with special courtesy, and the pleasantest relations prevailed. At six o'clock the polls closed and the slow, laborious count of a complicated paper ballot began. The new state constitution was on the ballot, and four other questions besides the suffrage amendment and a long list of candidates. The suffrage count came after these.

At headquarters, thronged by women, the figures coming in indicated from the first that suffrage had lost. Women were tired, their faces were drawn and white, but there were no tears, only a great determination. Suddenly, Mrs. Laidlaw, chairman of Manhattan Borough, sprang up, her head held high, her lovely color heightened:

"Who'll go with me now and start a new campaign with a street meeting?"

From all over the room came the response, and onto the street suffragists trouped. It was midnight or past, but the streets were still full of people. Soon the entire city knew that the suffrage fight was not ended. The first battle was lost but the campaign would continue until suffrage was won.

The morning after the election, all over the state, suffragists met and made plans for greatly increased activities, new workers appeared, new offers of help poured in. In spite of defeat the election gave women a sense of triumph. Half a million men had voted for woman suffrage, the largest number of votes suffragists had ever polled in one election. 700,000 men had voted against it, but 500,000 registered voters had not voted at all. If these men could be reached and converted another election would bring victory. That was our slogan, "Victory in 1917." Two days later, at a packed mass meeting in Cooper Union, which overflowed into the square, pledges of money and help came in a flood.

At the annual convention of the National American Woman Suffrage Association, early in December, Dr. Anna Howard Shaw, the president, resigned. With so many states won she believed that the national association should be directed by a president with keen political sense. The demand of the entire country that Mrs. Catt should lead the national campaign was overwhelming. Very reluctantly she took up the immense burden of trying to win the federal amendment. Mrs. Whitehouse, the first vice-chairman, therefore became chairman of the New York Woman Suffrage Party. The new chairman was young, beautiful, and brimful of energy. The treasurer, Mrs. Ogden Reid, was extraordinarily able. Together they surrounded themselves with a group of remarkable women, many of them new workers, young and enthusiastic.

A new campaign had been started but as yet there was no amendment. To get the state legislature to resubmit an amendment which had just been voted down was beyond all precedent. The leaders of both senate and assembly were bitter anti-suffragists, and were on record as determined that no new bill should pass. They did not know that before the amendment was even drafted the suffragists were quietly interviewing legislators getting their promises to vote for the measure. Senator Brown, chairman of the Senate Judiciary Committee, awoke with a shock one day to find that twelve of the thirteen members of his committee were pledged to vote for the amendment.

For months the bill went without action. Every week Mrs. Whitehouse and Mrs. Laidlaw, with other leaders, went to Albany. Mrs. Helen Leavitt, chairman of the legislative committee, never missed a session. Hearings were held and every effort made by the suffragists to influence their representatives. On March 14, the bill was passed by the assembly. On March 22, in spite of Senator Brown, the senate judiciary committee reported the bill favorably, but Senator Brown was determined. For over two weeks, day after day, he held the senate from acting, while he introduced one amendment after another. On each amendment a vote had to be taken, and the men were not pledged on these. They had promised only to vote for the suffrage bill. If any one of these amendments should pass the bill would be nullified.

Day after day the telephone booths at the Capitol were occupied by harassed and anxious women, calling up suffrage leaders in county after county. One after another a senator would be called up by the most influential men of his district, demanding that he stand firm. For eighteen long days and sleepless nights the women strove to outwit the most astute men of both political parties. Late at night, on April 10, the bill passed the senate, 33 to 10.

Meanwhile the assembly district organization was being pushed into every corner of the state. In addition all the special groups were greatly extended. The educational section, still under Mrs. Howard Mansfield, produced immense quantities of literature—appeals to every class of voters. During the final year of the campaign over eighteen million pieces of literature and suffrage novelties were distributed at a total cost to the campaign committee of less than $10,000.

The speakers' bureau, in charge of Mrs. Victor Morawetz, was a full time job. Congressmen and senators from suffrage states, prominent men in all walks of life, lent their aid, and hundreds of women were trained in speakers' schools.

Working women enlisted the help of the trade unions, and for the first time in the history of the labor movement women were given active official support.

From the beginning, both Mrs. Whitehouse and Mrs. Reid had determined on a campaign fund beyond anything suffragists had hitherto dreamed possible. For our first campaign, 1913-15, we had less than $90,000 for the entire state. Now each campaign district undertook to finance its own work, and in addition the chairman and treasurer set themselves the task of raising $300,000 for the central campaign committee. Such a great fund could not be obtained from suffragists alone, and they planned to raise money in the usual way of political parties, from wealthy men.

When, in February, 1917, the United States entered the World War, suffrage news, which up to this time had been filling the papers, was crowded out by war news. To keep the suffrage campaign before the public the two women decided that a newspaper advertising campaign was necessary, and that they must raise $200,000 more for that purpose.

How they did this is a story too long to tell here, but the figures as reported to the secretary of state give the result. The Woman Suffrage Party of the state raised $127,296.23, while the central campaign committee raised and spent $398,068.01. To this fund suffragists everywhere contributed, many with a generosity and self sacrifice beyond all praise. Not a penny of this money was used in any illegitimate way, and the only salaries paid were to a small group of organizers and office help.

In spite of the continued opposition of the legislative leaders, the suffrage bill passed for the second time. War or no war, the suffrage question was going to be voted on in the November election. Women must not lose again. With the United States engaged in a war for democracy, New York State could not afford to refuse democracy to its own women.

All through the spring and summer however, suffragists almost forgot their own campaign as they plunged into war work. The Woman Suffrage Party offered its services and was given definite tasks. Late in the summer suffrage leaders became alarmed at the disintegration of their organization. They made strenuous efforts to rally their scattered forces. It was up-hill work, but by the middle of September women threw themselves into the campaign as never before, and from that time the work went on with increasing momentum until election day.

The canvassing of women, especially, had almost stopped. Now it was pushed energetically, and soon suffragists proudly proclaimed, "1,030,800 New York women ask you to vote yes for woman suffrage on November 6th." Millions of leaflets gave the figures, they were printed in every newspaper, and great electric signs carried the message for every man to see.

During the final weeks every voter in the state was circularized with special literature. Special speakers were sent to the 150,000 New York soldiers in training camps. The soldiers in Europe had an absentee vote. Lists were obtained through the courtesy of the secretary of state, and a special appeal was sent to every man.

Early in September suffrage advertising began to appear everywhere. Huge street banners hung across the most crowded thoroughfares. Advertising was in theatre programs, in subway, elevated and surface cars. Small posters were in thousands of windows, and great ones on bill boards. Governor Charles A. Whitman gave open support and President Wilson urged voters to vote for the amendment.

In the final parade, the focus of interest was the lists of women asking for the vote. The signatures were carried for every one to see, an impressive demonstration—never again could men say "Women don't want to vote." The day after the parade newspapers carried in huge headlines a page of suffrage advertising, and every day until election the principal papers of the state carried appeals to voters to "Vote yes on amendment no. 1, on election day." It was an effective close to a great campaign.

Early in the fall the newspapers announced that thirty-four women had been appointed members of Tammany Hall and a few days before the election one of these brought a message to Mary Garrett Hay, Suffrage chairman of the City of New York, to the effect that Tammany would grant freedom to every voter to express his own convictions on the suffrage amendment at the polls. The few who learned of this message knew that victory was assured.

Nothing won more attention and respect from the politicians of all parties than the fact that 10,000 women, trained and equipped, were to take their places as watchers at the polls on election day.

Victory was in the air. Suffrage headquarters in the evening was thronged as in 1915, but this time the atmosphere was electric with hope and anticipation. The returns soon began to show that suffrage was winning in every borough in the city. Then the wires began to tell of major victories up-state and the excitement grew.

Some one rushed in: "The *Times* has just flashed a white light showing suffrage has carried the state." The women cheered and shouted, laughed and cried. Miss Hay, at the head of the big table, could not make herself heard and rapped with a rolling pin. Beside her sat Dr. Shaw, her face white with the strain of waiting, but her eyes shining. She was seeing her dream come true. Mrs. Catt gave the keynote:

"The victory is not New York's alone. It's the nation's. The 66th Congress is sure to pass our federal amendment."

Chapter X

The Winning Plan

Maud Wood Park

Chapter X

The Winning Plan

The plan which assured our final victory was made in 1916 by Mrs. Catt. She was convinced that the time had come for a federal amendment drive, although the ninety-one presidential electors for whom women could vote at that time were not enough to induce the Congress to submit the amendment. Her plan therefore called for the piling up of state victories until their cumulative effect proved irresistible.

The national association, of which she was then president, had grown to be a strong organization with headquarters in New York, forty-four state auxiliaries, made up of local branches, and a total membership of over two million. At a closed meeting of the executive council following the emergency convention in Atlantic City in September, 1916, she outlined the campaign, dividing the state auxiliaries into four groups and assigning to each a particular task.

First, the twelve states where women could vote for presidential electors were to secure from the next sessions of their legislatures resolutions asking the Congress to submit a woman suffrage amendment.

Second, the few states where there was a chance of carrying a state constitutional amendment were to try for that.

Third, the largest group of states was to work for presidential suffrage.

Fourth, southern states where the primary virtually determined the election were to try for primary suffrage.

As Mrs. Catt explained, work had to start at once in order to have everything ready at the beginning of the legislative sessions. The scope of the plan must not leak out, for, with simultaneous campaigns, the opposition, taken by surprise, might concentrate on a few states and thus hold out a sufficient number to cause defeat.

When we filed out of the room at the close of that meeting, I thought I understood how Moses felt on the mountain-top after he was shown the Promised Land. For the first time our goal looked possible of attainment in the near future.

Our state organizations did their work so well that before the 19th Amendment was adopted twenty-six legislatures sent resolutions to the Congress asking for the amendment; four states won constitutional amendments; thirteen legislatures granted presidential suffrage to women; two gave primary suffrage. In less than three years the number of presidential electors for whom women could vote jumped from 91 to 339.

When the drive began, our congressional committee was made up of fifteen members appointed by the national board of the suffrage association. These members were expected to spend most of their time in Washington. They served as an outpost of information and advice, keeping in close touch with our friends in the Congress and trying to

SPEAKER GILLETT OF THE HOUSE OF REPRESENTATIVES SIGNS SUFFRAGE BILL JUNE 5, 1919.

Left to Right:
  MRS. IDA HUSTED HARPER
  MRS. HARRIET TAYLOR UPTON
  MRS. MAUD WOOD PARK
  MISS MARY GARRETT HAY
  MRS. HELEN GARDENER
  MISS MARJORIE SHULER
  SPEAKER GILLETT, *of the House of Representatives*
  HON. JOHN E. RAKER, *former Chairman House Committee on Woman Suffrage*
  HON. CHAMP CLARK, *former Speaker*
  MR. TYLER PAGE, *Clerk of House of Representatives*
  HON. FRANK W. MONDELL, *Republican Floor Leader*

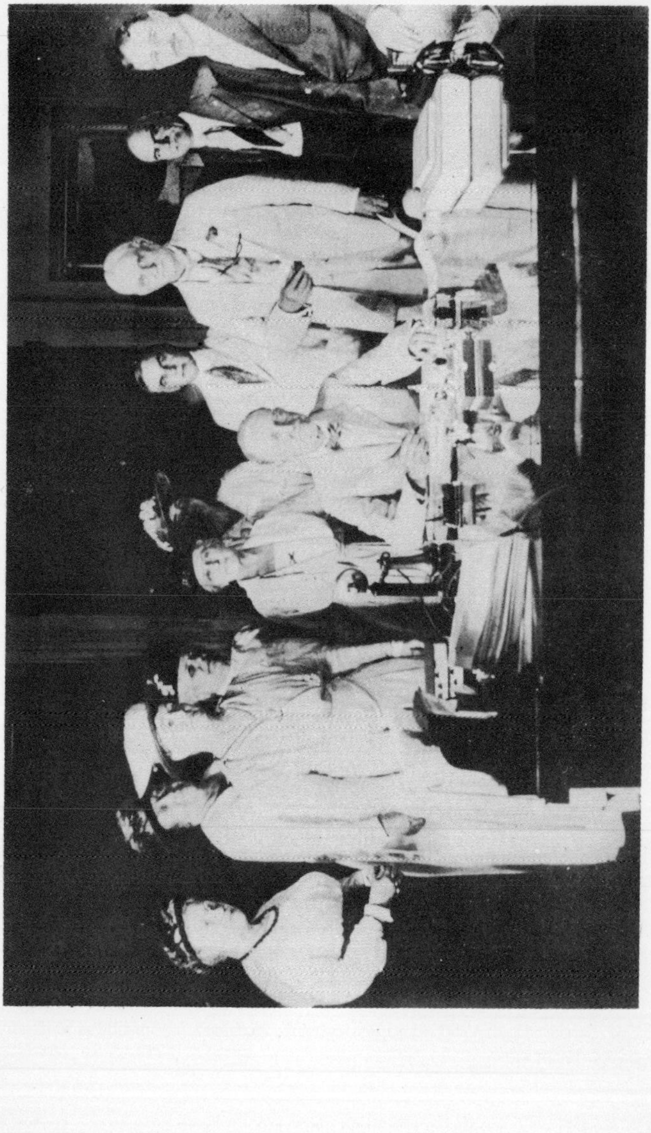

enlist the support of political and other leaders. This committee formed the nucleus of our lobby, the rest being suffragists summoned from the states for varying periods of time and for particular pieces of work. Our poll of the Congress was based on reports from the home districts of its members and was checked constantly by our Washington lobby. This last came to be known as "the front door lobby," a name given us by one of the press gallery men because we never used backstairs methods.

For the benefit of new workers we had drawn up detailed "Directions to Interviewers," later condensed into a few "Don'ts."

> Don't stay too long.
> Don't nag.
> Don't threaten.
> Don't talk about your work where you can be overheard.
> Don't draw out arguments against the Amendment.
> Don't do anything to close the door on the next advocate for suffrage.

Reports were written immediately after interviews and some of them were entertaining, for example:

"Representative ——— believes that woman dwells apart from man in her nature. She is different. Nature made it so. All history, science, biology prove it. Look at the barnyard, the cockerel protects the hen, etc. He deplored the lack of woman's trust in man, and did not think women wanted to be called 'suffragands' (correlation of the word brigands)."

The shortest report was that of an interview with Representative La Guardia of New York.

" 'I'm with you. I'm for it. I'm going to vote for it. Now don't bother me,' all in one breath."

When our vote was taken Mr. La Guardia was oversea in war service, but he cabled a request to be paired in favor.

Not a penny of salary was ever paid to members of our committee, or to those who helped in the lobby. Compared with the hundreds of thousands spent by some business lobbies our annual expenditure of about $24,000 was marvellously low. The Leslie fund had become available by this date, and the chief costs of the Congressional expenditures were borne by it.

When I joined the committee in 1916, Mrs. Walter McNab Miller was the chairman and Miss Ruth White the secretary. Their system of collecting data about every member of the Congress, and the method by which the committee was linked up with workers all over the country were impressive. Each of our state auxiliaries had a state congressional chairman, and under her were district chairmen for the congressional districts of her state. All of these were kept in close touch with our committee by bulletins and letters and, in times of emergency, by telegrams and long distance telephone. Congressional aides, ninety-five women chosen for their political influence made up another group. When we needed "backfires" in the district of a wobbly congressman, we called on our aides in his state to stir up publicity and to see that he heard from important constituents.

As soon as a state took favorable action on a suffrage measure, our congressional committee made a point of congratulating its senators and representatives. Then we called upon our staunch friends in both houses to urge them to bring up the good news in cloak rooms and other gathering places. Thus a belief in the inevitability of woman suffrage was built up. "Nothing succeeds like success."

No matter how urgent organization or legislative work might be, the education of public opinion was never lost sight of. Besides *The Woman Citizen,* the official organ of the association, numberless publications—fact sheets, arguments, foreign language fliers—were prepared in the national office and, in addition to the usual sorts of press work, there was a special service to furnish material about the amendment for editorial columns.

In January, 1917 a bill giving presidential and municipal suffrage to women was passed by the legislature of North Dakota. Senator McCumber of that state, a steadfast opponent, was an excellent illustration of the way state victories registered in the Congress. Before voting in favor of the amendment, he made an anti-suffrage speech containing this explanation:

"My own judgment is against this resolution . . . but the legislature of the state of North Dakota passed . . . an act which extended the right of suffrage to women . . . and I feel as a representative of the state I should vote their views rather than my own upon this subject."

Late in January came Germany's sudden notice of unrestricted submarine warfare. Overnight the shadow of the Great War fell on Washington. For the rest of the session woman suffrage, like every other issue not connected with the international situation, was in abeyance.

Before the new Congress met, Mrs. Miller, our committee chairman, resigned and I was appointed in her place. That responsibility I should not have dared to undertake if Mrs. Helen Gardener of Washington, for several years a member of the committee, had not agreed to be vice-chairman. We called her "the diplomatic corps" because her unusual tact made and kept so many important friends for the cause. She was one woman in whom the White House secretaries had complete confidence and to whom the President never refused an appointment. The work for which she had a superlative gift was necessarily confidential, but whenever at crucial moments aid came from high places so unexpectedly that it seemed miraculous, we knew Helen Gardener was responsible.

The other members of the committee at that time were Mrs. William Jennings Bryan, Nebraska; Mrs. Winston Churchill, New Hampshire; Mrs. Guilford Dudley, Tennessee; Mrs. Robert Griffin, Mrs. J. Borden Harriman and Miss Mary Garrett Hay, New York; Mrs. Medill McCormick, Illinois; Mrs. Charles McClure, Michigan; Miss Heloise Meyer and Miss Mabel Willard, Massachusetts; Mrs. Frank Roessing, Pennsylvania, Miss Ruth White, Missouri, and Miss Martha Norris, Ohio.

As soon as war measures started in the 65th Congress a "gentlemen's agreement" was made between party leaders to take up no general legislation until those measures were disposed of. All we could do for our amendment was to arrange for an early hearing before the Senate committee.

Meanwhile many of our workers had been called to war service, some of them oversea. Dr. Shaw was appointed chairman and Mrs. Catt and Mrs. Stanley McCormick, our vice-president, members of the Women's Committee of the Council for National Defense. The association itself took on heavy war responsibilities, including the maintenance of a hospital unit in France composed entirely of women. In the states hundreds of suffragists headed local committees. But the drive for suffrage never slackened.

A way out of the impasse due to the "gentleman's agreement" was suggested by Dr. McKelway, our adviser on procedure. "Try for a House committee on woman suffrage," he urged. "Creating a committee doesn't belong in the category of general legislation. It's a step in organization." Knowing that with such a committee we could count on a prompt report, and, if the chairman were favorable, on having the amendment come to the floor in the hands of a friend, we followed Dr. McKelway's suggestion. Our efforts were backed by the potent argument of presidential suffrage for women in five more states and primary suffrage in Arkansas. In eight months Mrs. Catt's plan had raised our total of electoral votes from 91 to 172.

The Arkansas triumph was particularly helpful because it marked our first break in the South. In 1914 and 1915 both Senators and all the representatives from that State had been recorded against the amendment. After the victory the entire delegation, including two new members and seven men who had previously voted "no," became supporters.

Our bill creating a woman suffrage committee passed, September 24, 1917, by a substantial majority, though far short of the two-thirds required to pass the amendment. Still we were jubilant over this first congressional victory.

That November New York's adoption of the state constitutional amendment sent our thermometer of electoral votes up to 217. To many doubters this was the "handwriting on the wall."

Nevertheless we began to hear an amazing rumor that the new Woman Suffrage Committee would not be permitted to have charge of our amendment because constitutional amendments had always come to the floor of the House through the Judiciary Committee. Believing Mr. Webb, the chairman of that committee, the source of the rumor, Helen Gardener and I went to consult one of our powerful friends in the House. To our horror he sustained Webb's claim.

"But why should we want a woman suffrage committee if it can't take charge of the amendment?"

"I don't know. You said you wanted a committee and I promised to help you get it, but I never told you it could handle the amendment."

I was about to say we had been tricked when a covert pinch from Mrs. Gardener checked me. As soon as we were out of the office, she explained. "He isn't double crossing us. He didn't know about this till Webb told him, but he'd rather have us think he didn't play fair than admit he was mistaken about House procedure. We'll need his help a good many times in the future and we can't afford to antagonize him now."

In sleepless hours that night I thought of looking up the history of the amendments already adopted. The Income Tax had come to the House through the Ways and Means Committee. My first impulse was to take this information to our backsliding friend, but "No," said Helen Gardener. "We mustn't let him think we know more than he does." So she arranged to have his secretary, with no sign of outside initiative, present the reference. After that none of our supporters backed Webb's claim, though he continued to press it until the Rules Committee reported the "rule" for debate on our resolution with the Woman Suffrage Committee in charge.

The date set for the vote on the amendment was January 10, 1918. While our lobby of women from seventeen states made the final check-up of our poll, we strove to secure the active cooperation of Republican and Democratic national leaders. We also persuaded fifty-one of our chief friends in the House to form a bi-partisan steering committee. It proved to be the one group in our experience in which members of both parties worked harmoniously. Their championship went a long way toward building up the conviction that the amendment had a real chance. Men who were still waiting to see which way the cat was likely to jump turned their heads a little further in our direction.

Early in January the last congressional hearings on woman suffrage were given by the new committee with Mr. Raker of California as chairman. Mrs. Catt and Dr. Shaw were the chief speakers for our association, which was heard the first day. The second was given to the National Woman's Party, and the third to the opponents, with Mrs. James Wadsworth, Jr., national president of the women's organization against suffrage, leading. On the last day we had a chance for rebuttal. Shortly afterwards the committee, made up of thirteen members, brought in a favorable report, only three dissenting.

Scores of women came to Washington for the vote and these we used for last minute interviews. Through the efforts of Representative Keating of Colorado, every known friend who could not be present was paired with an opponent on the basis of two in favor to one opposed. When the day came Representative Mann of Illinois left a hospital for the first time in months in order to help us. A New York member came from the deathbed of his wife, who had been an ardent suffragist. Representative Sims of Tennessee, refusing to have a broken shoulder set for fear of being kept away, stayed, in excruciating pain, until the vote was taken.

Jeannette Rankin opened the general debate in which there were forty speeches, twenty-three for, seventeen against. The chief argument of the opponents was state rights, particularly in connection with the Southern bugbear of Negro suffrage. The war was used by speakers on both sides. "We are engaged in a great foreign war. It is not the proper time to change the whole electoral system," said one, and another replied "There never was a more propitious time . . . than this hour for America to grant the right of suffrage to the noble women of this Republic."

When the triple agony of the roll call began, we started to check our poll. Before the names had been read through the first time we knew our victory hung by a thread. To get two affirmative votes for every negative was a terrific task. On the floor our friends were scurrying up and down the aisles and out to the coat rooms to get in for the second roll-call pledged members who had not answered the first time. Our opponents were scurrying too. Just below our gallery one of them was arguing with a man on our "doubtful" list.

As the second call started a stretcher was brought in and lying there unable to walk, Mr. Barnhart of Indiana voted "yes." When the second call ended the issue was still in doubt. The third call, the last opportunity, brought wild confusion around the speaker's desk. There were appeals and challenges, decisions by the Speaker, applause by our opponents.

Then, at long last came the announcement, 274 in favor, 136 opposed. On the floor our friends were cheering like mad. Men standing below shouted congratulations to us. Outside the gallery someone started "Praise God from Whom all blessings flow" and hundreds of women's voices took up the refrain.

Apparently we had two votes to spare, but if a single one of our supporters had gone over to the other side it would have taken two votes to offset his. In that case only the promise of the Speaker to have himself recorded if a single vote could save us, would have prevented defeat. The yeas were exactly 100 more than when the amendment had its previous vote. Of this number fifty-six were due to changes in the votes from the states where there had been recent suffrage victories—thirty of them from men who had voted "no" in 1915. Clearly it was state gains that carried us over the top.

Turning now to the Senate, our poll at that time showed fifty-four senators in favor, thirty-six opposed, and six, including vacancies, doubtful. Our problem was to get ten more supporters. After the number we lacked had been reduced several times by the filling of vacancies and the winning of a few doubtfuls, the death of friendly senators set us back again. During that Congress there were ten deaths in the Senate, seven of them in the ranks of our friends.

That winter we made increased use of Suffrage House as a gathering place for women in congressional circles. Mabel Willard, our chairman of social activities, was successful in getting as guests of honor at a series of teas many of the most prominent women in Washington. The wives of some of the opposed senators were frequent callers and their daughters often handed about our tea and cakes. Though we gained no votes that way, we removed many prejudices against women lobbyists.

By May, with the help of primary suffrage in Texas, which increased our electoral votes to 237 we were only two votes short in the Senate. When months had gone by without our gaining those two votes, Mrs. Catt called for mass meetings of protest throughout the country, with resolutions to the Senate requesting a favorable vote on the amendment. The resolutions literally poured in, with such organizations as the American Federation of Labor and the General Federation of Women's Clubs adding support.

More important were new political endorsements which we made every possible effort to secure. To maintain our non-partisan stand we were obliged to balance support by one party with some corresponding testimonial from the other. Neither party wanted its rival to have the monopoly of women's gratitude if and when the amendment went through. As our knowledge of the partisan attitude of the senators increased we hit upon the plan of having a steering committee of our own, in which Miss Hay, an avowed Republican, though not then in party office, was our Republican "steer" and Mrs. Guilford Dudley, well known as a Democrat, our Democratic "steer." When it seemed wise to have a strictly party approach to a man in public life, one of them did the interviewing. What they learned was reported to me with the understanding that the information would not be given to the representative of the other party. The job of go-between was a ticklish one, but it gave me an excellent training for our work with friends of both parties in the Senate.

At the end of the summer the two votes we needed were still lacking, but we decided that in any case we must have a Senate vote before the election. Senator Jones of New Mexico, whose committee had brought in the first unanimously favorable report on the amendment, arranged to bring it up on September 25th. Most of our congressional friends were hopeful that the efforts of the President and some of the Republican leaders, and the nearness of the election would give us the necessary number, but, as the day approached, the most promising possibilities faded away. Again women from a distance flocked to Washington. Although we tried to make them realize we were still two short they could not believe that we could fail by such a small number. Their high hopes were registered in the diary kept by Rose Young, which began:

"Suffrage House, September 24. For the last time the old bodyguard is here. For the last time the trains are hourly bringing in women from all parts of the country—women who are leaving war work just long enough to rush here for the final round-up. . . .

"Mrs. Catt has been here for weeks. Mrs. Park is always here. So is Mrs. Gardener. Miss Hay is here, proud of the Republicans. Mrs. Dudley is here, confident of the Democrats. . . . There are not many states in the Union unrepresented by one or more prominent women. By Friday, Dr. Shaw of the United States will be here.

"All the talk is of victory."

The five day debate started on the 26th, with opponents basing their arguments largely on state rights. By the third day the talk at Suffrage House was no longer of victory. Sunday morning Mrs. Catt sent a letter asking the President to address the Senate in behalf of the amendment. That afternoon two friends, Senator Shafroth and Senator Pittman, went to the White House and we waited in anxiety until word came that the President would take the almost unprecedented step of addressing the Senate upon a measure that required the vote of both Houses. He spoke on Monday, closing with the plea:

"I tell you plainly as commander in chief of our armies and of the gallant men of our fleets . . . as the guide and director of forces caught in the grip of war and by the same token in need of every material and spiritual resource this great nation possesses—I tell you plainly that the measure which I urge upon you is vital to the winning of the war and to the energies alike of preparation and of battle."

Perhaps if the vote had been taken immediately the result might have been different. But as soon as the President left the Chamber opposed senators began to refute his arguments and to rattle once more the dry bones of state rights objections. Our chief enemies moved about the floor to see whether their forces were still unbroken. The two floor leaders, Lodge of Massachusetts and Martin of Virginia, were arm in arm comparing notes—"the unholy alliance" we called them.

So the afternoon dragged on. We felt as if we were at a funeral, awaiting the arrival of the clergyman. The next day there was little left but the interment. The vote, including pairs, was sixty-two in favor and thirty-four against. Every senator was accounted for. We had lost by two votes of the required sixty-six. The President's appeal had not changed a single vote.

Our next battle ground was chosen the day after the defeat. We had to see that at least two unfriendly senators were not re-elected. The first choice fell on Senator Weeks, Republican, of Massachusetts, and Senator Saulsbury, Democrat, of Delaware. Two others, Senator Baird of New Jersey and Moses, the hostile nominee in New Hampshire, were included by our national board. Against these two pairs the National Woman's Party also launched an attack. Although Weeks was held to be impregnable, our non-partisan committee of Massachusetts women organized their campaign so strategically that he was defeated by a substantial majority. Saulsbury, too, was defeated. Baird and Moses were elected but with reduced majorities.

The election assured us of victory in the 66th Congress, but there was still the short session of the 65th ahead. For that we had a new friend in Senator Pollock of South Carolina and, as the Republicans were to control the new Congress, we thought the Democrats would not let their last chance of credit for passing the amendment go for lack of one vote.

In the weeks that followed it seemed to me that everybody in the United States knew we were just one short. One afternoon when I went back to Suffrage House, after hearing several unfavorable reports from senators who were trying to help us, I found a young woman waiting for me with a letter of introduction.

"I've come" she explained, "because I've heard that you understand lobbying, and I thought I'd like to be with you when you crack some tough old nut of a senator to get that last vote."

I was too exasperated to be polite. "Young lady," I said, "sixty-three senators, both national party committees, cabinet members and the President of the United States have thus far been unable to get that one vote. If I knew how to do it do you suppose I should have waited for you to go with me?"

Early in February our friends concluded that further delay might jeopardize our chance of action before final adjournment. So on February 10, 1919, Senator Jones again brought up the amendment. We lost by just one vote.

That meant beginning all over again with the 66th Congress. By the time it met six more states had given presidential suffrage to women and our electoral thermometer stood at 326. In the House Mr. Mann, new chairman of the Woman Suffrage Committee, managed to get a vote on our resolution on the third day of the session, May 21st.

Sitting in the gallery while the debate went on we scarcely recognized our cause in its setting of gaiety. No scurrying for another vote, no sick men coming in to be recorded, Democratic opponents repeatedly congratulating Republicans on their celerity in jumping on the band wagon. From time to time gusts of laughter greeted the "yes" of a man who had voted "no" sixteen months before. We won by 304 to 89, thirty-four votes to spare.

But there was still the Senate. Maine's presidential suffrage victory had assured us of Senator Hale's vote, and the President's interest brought promise of a vote from Georgia, these in addition to the two we had won in the election. The roll-call on June 4th gave us, with pairs included, 66 to 30, two more than the necessary two-thirds. Among our supporters that day were five senators who had previously voted a "no," but who changed to our side because of suffrage gains in their states. Again state victories proved the deciding factor.

Vice President Marshall, an opponent, gave the chair to Senator Cummins of Iowa, our long time friend, to make the announcement. His voice trembled as he said:

"The joint resolution having received the affirmative vote of more than two-thirds of the senators present and voting, is declared to have passed the Senate in accordance with the Constitution of the United States."

The fifty-three years' fight in the Congress was won.

Chapter XI

The Secretary Has Signed the Proclamation

Mary Gray Peck

Chapter XI

The Secretary Has Signed the Proclamation

The 19th Amendment passed the Congress at five o'clock in the afternoon of June 4, 1919. Mrs. Catt was in New York where the suffrage headquarters were located, and within the hour she had launched the campaign for ratification. Telegrams were sent to the governors of all states where ratification would require the calling of special sessions, urging them to call such sessions. The first favorable responses came from Governors Al Smith of New York and Henry Allen of Kansas, and were soon followed by a dozen others. Besides these, several governors gave conditional promises. A few days after the first telegram, a second was sent which brought some additional favorable replies.

In less than a week after it was submitted, the amendment was ratified by Illinois and Wisconsin whose legislatures were in regular session. On the same day, June 10, Michigan ratified, having called the legislature in special session in time to come in neck and neck with the first two states. Three more states, Kansas and New York in special session, Ohio in regular, ratified on June 16—six ratifications inside of as many days. Pennsylvania, Massachusetts and Texas followed in quick succession, making nine ratifications in June. For a detailed account of state ratifications, most of which had extremely interesting stories, the reader is referred to "Woman Suffrage and Politics," written by Mrs. Catt and Nettie R. Shuler.

July brought three ratifications, Iowa, Missouri and Arkansas. Montana and Nebraska ratified in August; after which the initial rush of ratifications slackened. Things were not going according to the suffrage schedule, which had assumed that the equal suffrage states would take the lead in ratifying, while the opposition would make its stand in the conservative east. Just the opposite was taking place; not a state in the far west had ratified while Pennsylvania and Massachusetts were among the earliest to do so. In fact the Pennsylvania legislature had burst into joyful song after it voted! In contrast to this generous spirit the far western governors with one accord kept making excuse for not calling special sessions.

Four envoys were sent out by the National Suffrage Association in the middle of the summer to labor with these men and to appeal to the annual conference of governors which met in Salt Lake City, that year. In response, they secured public pledges from seven governors, private pledges from three. September saw Minnesota, New Hampshire and Utah bring the ratifications up to seventeen.

In October, Mrs. Catt accompanied by a troupe of suffrage speakers started on a tour of the far western states with the purpose of stirring up the women about ratification. The governors of most of these states saw no reason for haste since their women had the vote. Why not wait till the legislatures met in regular session to ratify? Nothing but pressure from their own constituents could make them see that their indifference was slowing down the whole program and would prevent women from voting on a national scale in the 1920 election. The suffrage mission toured twelve far western states, and as a result, California, North and South Dakota, and Colorado ratified in special sessions, while in the far east Maine took similar action. The end of 1919 saw the amendment ratified by twenty-two states.

January of 1920 brought five ratifications—Rhode Island, Kentucky, Oregon, Indiana and Wyoming; February rolled up six—Nevada, New Jersey, Idaho, Arizona, New Mexico and Oklahoma. Ratification by Oklahoma cost the life of Miss Aloysius Larch-Miller, devoted secretary of the women's ratification committee. A political convention was to be addressed by one of the ablest orators in the state, who was opposing a special session for ratification. Against the orders of her physician, she went to the convention and urged ratification in a speech which carried the delegates with her. Two days later, she died.

Thirty-three states were now in the ratification column, but let it not be supposed that the anti-suffrage forces had been doing nothing all this time. The wets were determined to overthrow the recently enacted prohibition amendment, and to prevent ratification of the suffrage amendment which they considered almost as bad. Powerful manufacturing interests were allied with them. These business interests had plenty of money and they adopted a new method of attack. Twenty-two states had initiative and referendum provisions in their constitutions—Ohio being among the number. The ratification of the prohibition amendment had been referred to the voters and defeated in an Ohio election, and the Ohio Supreme Court had declared the referendum constitutional. The anti-suffrage forces now began to circulate petitions for a similar referendum on the suffrage amendment ratification, with a view to nullifying it. Petitions for a referendum on the suffrage ratification were circulating in three other states and threatened elsewhere. Two state supreme courts declared such referenda constitutional, two declared they were not constitutional, and six were trying to make up their minds. Here was a legal situation which might tie up ratification indefinitely.

Foreseeing just this kind of an attempt to sabotage the 19th Amendment in the courts, the National American Woman Suffrage Association had retained former Supreme Court Justice Charles Evans Hughes as counsel. A number of cases challenging the validity of state referenda on the ratification of federal amendments were pending in the United States Supreme Court.

This was the situation with the advent of March, 1920; the opposition was fighting with all its force to recall ratifications already obtained, and to defeat ratification in the three states still needed to place the amendment in the Federal Constitution. The suffragists were staking everything they had to keep their thirty-three ratifications and get three more. Governor Cornwall had called the West Virginia legislature in special session, and the house voted to ratify by a majority of five. The senate vote was a tie! One of the senators, Jesse Bloch, who favored ratification, was in California, and the opposition refused to let him be paired, whereupon he flew back home and got there in time to break the tie and carry the amendment.

A few days after West Virginia, the State of Washington ratified in a unanimous vote—the thirty-fifth state. Only one more ratification needed!

Carrie Chapman Catt

Carrie Chapman Catt

Carrie Lane was born in Ripon, Wisconsin, January 9, 1859, of colonial New England ancestry. She grew up on a farm near Charles City, Iowa; earned her way through Iowa State College; taught school and became Superintendent of Schools in Mason City, Iowa; married Leo Chapman, 1885, and after his death married George W. Catt, 1890.

She turned by instinct to the suffrage movement and in 1890 became identified with the National American Woman Suffrage Association. Her extraordinary genius for leadership caused Susan B. Anthony to choose Mrs. Catt to succeed her in the presidency when the old leader retired in 1900.

Mrs. Catt was a tireless organizer and campaigner. In 1909, she reorganized the suffrage forces on election district lines, giving political structure to the movement. After directing the first New York suffrage campaign, she was drafted in 1915 to lead the drive for the Federal Amendment. For five years the climactic struggle was waged with ever growing intensity. Two million organized women took part under Mrs. Catt's direction in the National American Woman Suffrage Association. Bitterly contested to the last ditch, the Nineteenth Amendment was ratified, August 26, 1920.

Her international activities were equally notable. She founded the International Woman Suffrage Alliance in 1902 and was its first president, retiring in 1923. She visited every continent and brought the women of all races into the movement.

Her late years have been devoted to the cause of international peace and disarmament. In 1925, she brought the leading national women's organizations together in the Conference on the Cause and Cure of War and later helped form the National Peace Conference.

MARY GRAY PECK

Governor Townsend of Delaware called his legislature in special session, and the legislators wrangled for two months before coming to the point. The senate then voted for ratification and the house voted not to vote on it at all!

Mississippi was another state where the senate favored and the house opposed ratification. There was great turbulence during the balloting, but one representative managed to make himself heard down the ages when he howled, "I would rather die and go to Hell than vote for woman suffrage!"

A mighty effort was made to get Governor Holcomb to call a special session in Connecticut, where the legislature had been polled and was known to be favorable. Mrs. Catt invited forty-six good speakers from as many states, to come to Connecticut where Miss Katherine Ludington, president of the Woman Suffrage Association, arranged mass meetings for them at which resolutions were passed urging the Governor to convene the legislature. The Governor stedfastly refused. After thirty-six ratifications had made Connecticut's action superfluous, the Governor then summoned the legislature and the latter ratified not once, but twice!

Governor Clement of Vermont likewise resisted every attempt to get action in that state. It, like Connecticut, waited till after the proclamation to ratify. There remained only Florida, North Carolina and Tennessee where action had not been taken, and of these only Tennessee offered any favorable prospect.

During May and June, Mrs. Catt was in Europe in connection with the post-war congress of the International Woman Suffrage Alliance. On her return, news was received from Tennessee that Governor Roberts had promised to convene the legislature for special session in August. The Tennessee suffragists sent Mrs. Catt an urgent appeal to come to their aid. She went, thinking to stay a few days. She remained there during the last and most harrowing six weeks of the whole seventy-two years that women had to fight for the ballot in these "free and equal" United States.

The same legislature that the preceding year had granted Tennessee women the presidential suffrage, would act on ratification. The state constitution stipulated that after the submission of a federal amendment, a new legislature must be elected before voting on ratification. True, the United States Supreme Court had decreed that the federal constitution took precedence over a state constitution when the two conflicted, but being south of the Mason and Dixon Line the Tennessee mind inclined to go along with its own charter.

In addition to the constitutional conflict, Governor Roberts, who was up for re-election in the fall, had a violent quarrel within the state Democratic party on his hands, while a similar split in the Republican party completed the political chaos. These factional animosities naturally were reflected in the suffrage ranks, and Mrs. Catt's first concern was to unite all suffragists in singleminded support of ratification. The Tennessee leaders were women of brilliant parts. Two of them, Mrs. Guilford Dudley and Miss Della Dortch, were officers of the National League of Women Voters, while Mrs. George Fort Milton was chairman of the Tennessee League of Women Voters. Mrs. Leslie Warner, who had led the campaign for presidential suffrage, Mrs. John Kenny, chairman of the Ratification Committee, and

HOW WOMEN WON IT

many others had built up a strong state suffrage organization.

As soon as Mrs. Catt arrived in the state, she started with Mrs. George Fort Milton on an extended speaking tour. They began in Memphis and ended in eastern Tennessee, visiting all the large cities, holding campaign conferences and mass meetings. It was July of one of the hottest summers on record, but Mrs. Catt had two ideas to bring to public attention: first, that the alleged conflict between state and federal constitutions had been ended by the decision of the Supreme Court, second, that the women of Tennessee were opposed by a sinister combination of the whiskey lobby, the manufacturers' lobby and the railroad lobby.

In a little village named Niota, in McMinn County in eastern Tennessee, an elderly woman read the reports of Mrs. Catt's speeches attentively. Perhaps she heard her speak. She had a son who had been recently elected to the lower house of the legislature, and she made him promise that if his vote were needed for ratification in the special session, he would give it. The mother's name was Mrs. J. L. Burn, and her son's name was Harry. They should both be remembered.

There was great interest on the part of the dominant national political parties in the approaching session of the Tennessee legislature. Both national committees in public statements urged ratification. Both presidential candidates, Governor Cox and Senator Harding sent Mrs. Catt personal letters expressing support. The Democratic national committee sent Miss Charl Williams, vice chairman of the Committee, to Nashville to represent them; the Republican national committee sent their vice chairman, Mrs. Harriet Taylor Upton. There were Democratic and Republican state committees of women for ratification, the Governor appointed his own ratification committee, the Woman's Party had a ratification committee with Miss Sue White as chairman. In view of so many committees, it was decided to have them choose a general chairman, and Miss Charl Williams was chosen for the responsible position. It was further decided that only Tennessee women should lobby at the Capitol.

The anti-suffragists also assembled in Nashville as the time for the special session arrived. Everett P. Wheeler had changed the name of his Men's Anti-Suffrage Association to the higher sounding title, American Constitutional League. He now formed a branch which took in some influential politicians who labored to detach men pledged to ratification. The activities of this organization were so questionable that a grand jury investigation was ordered.

The women's anti-suffrage societies were there, decked with red roses and interviewing legislators. Side by side with these old antagonists were two former officers of the national suffrage association who had worked for years under Susan B. Anthony and side by side with Mrs. Catt and Mrs. Upton, but who now were against ratification because they believed suffrage should come through state action only.

Many legislators put up at the Hermitage Hotel, and when they arrived they made their way by some mysterious instinct to a room on the eighth floor. When they reappeared, they were noticeably unsteady on their legs! In the chapter on Tennessee in "Woman Suffrage and Politics,"

Mrs. Catt writes, "Hour after hour, men and women who went to the different hotels of the city to talk with the legislators, came back to the Hermitage headquarters to report, and every report told the same story—the legislature was drunk!" However they slept it off during the night, and on Monday, the 9th of August, 1920, they were ready for business.

Four days after assembling, the senate voted, 24 to 4, in favor of ratification. In the house, the speaker, Seth Walker, who was a member of the women's ratification committee and had promised to introduce the measure himself, suddenly turned around and became the leader of the opposition! Before coming to Nashville, sixty-two members of the house had given written pledges to vote for ratification; as soon as they got there, one after another fell away to the other side, until the house was evenly divided. The suffragists now systematically shadowed their pledged legislators. If they saw one walk through the lobby with a bag in his hand, they asked where he was going. They picketed the railway stations and the committee rooms; they kept taking polls. Their pressure on the opposition was equally unremitting, and it is not strange that by the second week the legislature began to show signs of cracking. The women were determined to reclaim two votes before the house voted, otherwise their cause was lost in Tennessee.

Meantime, back in Niota, in the mountains of East Tennessee, Mrs. J. L. Burn eagerly scanned the papers to see what was happening down in Nashville to the 19th

Amendment. She was not pleased with what she read, and she wrote young Harry to that effect as follows:

"Dear Son:

Hurrah and vote for suffrage! Don't keep them in doubt. I notice some of the speeches against. They were bitter. I have been watching to see how you stood, but have not noticed anything yet. Don't forget to be a good boy and help Mrs. Catt put 'rat' in ratification.

Your Mother."

Wednesday of the second week, the house convened with the determination to end the deadlock. There was a last turgid debate, terminated by Speaker Walker who cried, "The hour has come! The battle has been fought and won!"—and moved to table the resolution. The roll-call began amid tense excitement. When it reached the letter T, a wild outcry shook the Capitol. Banks Turner had dropt off the fence on the suffrage side and the vote was a tie— 48 to 48! Unwilling to believe his ears, Walker called for a second roll-call, rushed to Turner's chair, threw his arm around him and poured frenzied entreaties into his ear. The second roll-call reached Turner's name, there was an agonizing pause, then Turner threw off Walker's arm and shouted, "No!" The vote to table had failed to carry and the vote now must be taken on ratification itself.

With sinking hearts the suffragists heard the roll-call begin, for a tie this time meant the defeat of ratification. Then came the prodigious moment. The clerk's monotonous voice called, "Harry Burn," for the third time that day, and Harry for the third time called back, "Aye," but this time the whole house broke into an uproar that was heard for blocks around the Capitol, for young Harry was keeping his promise to his mother and giving the 19th Amendment the one vote necessary to put it into the Federal Constitution.

Space is lacking to tell of the desperate efforts to overturn the ratification, culminating in the flight of thirty-eight anti-suffragist legislators in the night over the state line into Alabama in an attempt to destroy a quorum. The ratification certificate was signed by Governor Roberts with an injunction hanging over his head, and was sent by registered mail to the Secretary of State in Washington. It was received at the State Department at four o'clock in the morning, Thursday August 26, 1920, was referred at once to the Solicitor General who had been waiting up all night to certify its correctness, was returned to the State Department, and at eight o'clock that same morning, Secretary of State Bainbridge Colby signed the proclamation of the Woman Suffrage Amendment to the Federal Constitution, with nobody present but his secretary to see him do it.

The reason for all this nocturnal vigil and early rising was because of the extraordinary threats against the amendment. Mrs. Catt reached Washington that morning. She went to suffrage headquarters and called up the Department of State on the telephone. Maud Wood Park and Harriet Taylor Upton were with her in the room when she inquired if the Tennessee certificate had reached the Secretary of State? After a moment, she turned and said, "The Secretary has signed the proclamation. He invites us to come over and look at it!"

She hung up the receiver and leaned against the wall. The three women looked at one another in silence.

There was a great mass meeting in Washington that night. Next day Mrs. Catt, Charl Williams and Harriet

Taylor Upton went on to New York. At every stop they were met by victory delegations. When they rolled into the Pennsylvania station in New York, they were welcomed by Governor Al Smith and Senator Calder and a great crowd with the 71st Regiment band. Then, escorted by a guard of honor they were placed at the head of a marching column, and so with music playing and flags flying, the last suffrage parade passed through New York into history.

Appendix 1
BIBLIOGRAPHY

History of Woman Suffrage, Susan B. Anthony, Elizabeth Cady Stanton, Matilda Joslyn Gage, Ida Husted Harper, 6 vols., Fowler & Wells

Woman Suffrage and Politics, Carrie Chapman Catt and Nettie R. Shuler, Scribner, 1923

Life and Letters of James and Lucretia Mott, A. D. Hallowell, Houghton Mifflin, Boston, 1884

Life and Works of Susan B. Anthony, 3 vols., I. H. Harper

Eighty Years and More, Elizabeth Cady Stanton, European Publishing Co., N.Y., 1898?

Lucy Stone, Pioneer of Women's Rights, Alice Stone Blackwell, Little Brown, Boston, 1930

Story of a Pioneer, Anna Howard Shaw, Harper, N.Y., 1915

The Grimké Sisters, Catharine H. Birney, Lee and Shepard, Boston, 1885

Life of Mary Lyon, Beth Gilchrist, Houghton Mifflin, Boston, 1910

Woman Suffrage, History, Arguments, Results, Francis M. Bjorkman and Annie G. Porritt, National Woman Suffrage Publishing Co., N.Y., 1917

Letters of John Adams and His Wife, Abigail Adams During the Revolution. Hurd and Houghton, 1876

Father Shipherd's Magna Charta, Francis Juliette Horsford, Marshall, Jones Co., Boston, 1937?

Brief History of the Condition of Women in Various Ages and Nations, Lydia Maria Child, 2 vols. Francis, N.Y., 1832

Vindication of the Rights of Woman, Mary Wollstonecraft, Scribner and Welford, 1892

Emile, or Treatise on Education, Rousseau, W. H. Payne, tr. Appleton, N.Y., 1893

The First Woman Jury, Grace Raymond Hebard, Journal of American History, 1913, no.4

The Presidential Vote, E. E. Robinson, Leland Stanford University Press, 1934

Life of Emma Willard, Alma Lutz, Boston, Houghton Mifflin, 1929

Susan B. Anthony, R. E. C. Dorr, Frederick Stokes Company, 1928

The Greatest American Woman, Lloyd C. M. Hare, American Historical Society, 1937

Created Equal, Alma Lutz, John Day Company, 1940

Challenging Years, Harriot Stanton Blatch and Alma Lutz, G. P. Putnam's Sons, 1940

Files of *The Revolution, The Woman's Journal, The Woman Citizen*

Reports, letters and other data in files of National American Woman Suffrage Association.

Appendix 2

THE NATIONAL AMERICAN WOMAN SUFFRAGE ASSOCIATION

Organization for the purpose of removing the eighteen grievances listed at the Seneca Falls Convention of 1848 began with clubs, committees and conventions, scattered and disconnected. These efforts had so far been unified and directed that ten consecutive National annual conventions had been held before the Civil War, the last in Cooper Union, New York, in 1860. The war, as usual, brought women's efforts to an end and when, in 1866, the next convention was called, new problems had developed from the war which split the suffrage forces and demanded a new plan of procedure. The differences concerned the 14th and 15th Amendments. Some contended that women should be enfranchised before the negroes, some that negroes should be enfranchised before women, and others that women and negroes should be enfranchised at the same time. By 1869 the disputes had somewhat abated and enthusiasm over the woman's rights program had steadily increased. Therefore permanent organization was effected, but in two groups. The National Woman Suffrage Association was led by Elizabeth Cady Stanton and Susan B. Anthony; the American Woman Suffrage Association was led by Lucy Stone and her husband, Henry B. Blackwell. There was room for both and in only a few states did they interfere with each other. After working apart for twenty years these two groups, both grown larger and abler, merged in the National American Woman Suffrage Association in 1890 with Elizabeth Cady Stanton as president and Lucy Stone as chairman of the Executive Committee. Altho Susan B. Anthony led on for another ten years, the work of the Pioneers as a whole practically closed with the merger and another generation inherited the organization and the unfinished task.

The break in the forces at the date of the Civil War undoubtedly checked the progress of the movement, but the marvel is that from beginning to end the leadership remained intact, the aim unchanged and the Federal Amendment ratified in 1920 was precisely the same as when it was written in 1868.

The National American Woman Suffrage Association is an incorporated body and remains intact. It has had four presidents.

    1890-1892   Elizabeth Cady Stanton
    1892-1900   Susan B. Anthony
    1900-1904   Carrie Chapman Catt
    1904-1915   Dr. Anna Howard Shaw
    1915-   Carrie Chapman Catt

THE BOARD OF OFFICERS IN JULY 1940 ARE:

Carrie Chapman Catt, *President*
Mrs. Stanley McCormick, Illinois, *First Vice-President*
Mrs. Herbert Knox Smith, Connecticut, *Second Vice-President*
Mrs. Guilford Dudley, Tennessee, *Third Vice-President*
Mrs. Raymond Brown, New York, *Fourth Vice-President*
Maud Wood Park, Maine, *Fifth Vice-President*
Mabel Russell, New York, *Treasurer*
Mrs. Halsey W. Wilson, New York, *Recording Secretary*

THE BOARD OF DIRECTORS:

Mrs. J. C. Cantrill, Kentucky
Mrs. Richard E. Edwards, Indiana
Mrs. George Gelhorn, Missouri
Mrs. Alfred G. Lewis, New York
Miss Esther G. Ogden, Massachusetts
Mrs. George A. Piersol, Florida
Mrs. F. Louis Slade, New York
Mrs. Harriet Taylor Upton, California

The National Headquarters, 1624 Grand Central Terminal Building, 70 East 45th Street, New York City.

Appendix 3

INTERESTING EVENTS IN THE WOMAN'S RIGHTS MOVEMENT

- 1636   Ann Hutchinson's prayer meetings in Boston
- 1647   Margaret Brent's demand for a voice in the State Assembly, Maryland
- 1776   Abigail Adams' letter to John Adams, asking consideration of women in the laws of the new nation
- 1776-1807   Women taxpayers voted in New Jersey
- 1792   Publication of Mary Wollstonecraft's "Vindication of the Rights of Women"
- 1821   Emma Willard opened Troy Seminary
- 1826   Frances Wright's lectures on political topics
- 1826   High School for girls, Boston, opened
- 1828   High School for girls, Boston, closed
- 1828-1837   Grimke sisters' lectures on slavery
- 1832   Publication Lydia Maria Child's "History of Woman"
- 1833   Opening of Oberlin College
- 1836   Ernestine L. Rose's lectures on government
- 1837   Opening of Mt. Holyoke Seminary
- 1838   Mary Grove Nichols' lectures on anatomy
- 1838   Kentucky granted school suffrage to widows with children and property.
- 1840   Rejection of woman delegates from the United States by the anti-slavery convention at London
- 1840   Publication of Margaret Fuller's "Great Lawsuit" in The Dial
- 1841   Three women graduated at Oberlin with degrees, the first in the world to achieve this honor

VICTORY

1844 Paulina Wright Davis' lectures on physiology
1848 Elizabeth Blackwell graduated from Geneva Medical College
1848 At this date five states, Connecticut 1809, Ohio 1835, Texas 1840, Illinois 1845, Vermont 1849, had given to married women the right to make a will and Maine in 1844 had given married women the right to control their own property, but not the right to make a will and no married woman could yet legally collect and use her own wages.
1848 First Woman's Rights Convention, July, Seneca Falls, New York
1850 Second Woman's Rights Convention, April, Salem, Ohio
1850 First National Woman's Rights Convention, October, Worcester, Mass.
1850 Ordination of Antoinette Brown Blackwell as a Congregational minister
1852 High School for Girls, Boston, reopened

Appendix 4

THE ELECTORAL THERMOMETER

Woman Suffrage Won by State Constitutional Amendments and Legislative Acts Before the Proclamation of the 19th Amendment

		ELECTORAL VOTE
1890	WYOMING was admitted to statehood with woman suffrage, having had it as a territory since 1869.	3
1893	COLORADO adopted a constitutional amendment after defeat in 1877.	6
1896	IDAHO adopted a constitutional amendment on its first submission.	4
1896	UTAH after having woman suffrage as a territory since 1870 was deprived of it by the Congress in 1887, but by referendum put it back in the constitution when admitted to statehood.	4
1910	WASHINGTON adopted a constitutional amendment after defeats in 1889 and 1898. It had twice had woman suffrage by enactment of the territorial legislature and lost it by court decisions.	7
1911	CALIFORNIA adopted a constitutional amendment after defeat in 1896.	13
1912	OREGON adopted a constitutional amendment after defeats in 1884, 1900, 1906, 1908, 1910.	5
1912	KANSAS adopted a constitutional amendment after defeats in 1867 and 1893.	10
1912	ARIZONA adopted a constitutional amendment submitted as a result of referendum petitions.	3

VICTORY

ELECTORAL VOTE

1913 ILLINOIS was the first state to get presidential suffrage by legislative enactment. — 29

1914 MONTANA adopted a constitutional amendment on its first submission. — 4

1914 NEVADA adopted a constitutional amendment on its first submission. — 3

1917 NORTH DAKOTA secured presidential suffrage by legislative enactment, after defeat of a constitutional amendment in 1914. — 5

1917 NEBRASKA secured presidential suffrage by legislative enactment after defeats of a constitutional amendment in 1882 and 1914. — 8

1917 RHODE ISLAND secured presidential suffrage by legislative enactment after defeat of a constitutional amendment in 1887. — 5

1917 NEW YORK adopted a constitutional amendment after defeat in 1915. — 45

1917 ARKANSAS secured primary suffrage by legislative enactment. — 9

1918 MICHIGAN adopted a constitutional amendment after defeats in 1874, 1912 and 1913. Secured presidential suffrage by legislative enactment in 1917. — 15

1918 TEXAS secured primary suffrage by legislative enactment. — 20

1918 SOUTH DAKOTA adopted a constitutional amendment after six prior campaigns for suffrage had been defeated, each time by a mobilization of the alien vote by American-born political manipulators. In that state, as in nine others in 1918, the foreign-born could vote on their "first papers" and citizenship was not a qualification for the vote. The last defeat, in 1916, had been so definitely proved to have been

ELECTORAL VOTE

caused by the vote of German-Russians in nine counties that public sentiment, in addition to the war spirit, aroused a desire to make a change in the law which resulted in victory.   5

1918 OKLAHOMA adopted a constitutional amendment after defeat in 1910.   10

1919 INDIANA secured presidential suffrage by legislative enactment in 1917. Rendered doubtful by a court decision the law was re-enacted with but six dissenting votes.   15

1919 MAINE secured presidential suffrage by legislative enactment after defeat of a constitutional amendment in 1917.   6

1919 MISSOURI secured presidential suffrage by legislative enactment after defeat of a constitutional amendment in 1914.   18

1919 IOWA secured presidential suffrage by legislative enactment after defeat of a constitutional amendment in 1916.   13

1919 MINNESOTA secured presidential suffrage by legislative enactment.   12

1919 OHIO secured presidential suffrage by legislative enactment after defeat of referendum on the law in 1917 and of a constitutional amendment in 1912 and 1914.   24

1919 WISCONSIN secured presidential suffrage by legislative enactment after defeat of a constitutional amendment in 1912.   13

1919 TENNESSEE secured presidential suffrage by legislative enactment.   12

		ELECTORAL VOTE
1920	KENTUCKY secured presidential suffrage by legislative enactment.	13

Total of presidential electors for whom women were entitled to vote before the 19th Amendment was adopted, 339. (Full number 531)

In 1913 the territory of Alaska had adopted woman suffrage. It was the first bill approved by the Governor.

Appendix 5

PARTIAL SUFFRAGE GAINS

School Suffrage

- 1838 Kentucky, for widows with children of school age in country districts
- 1861 Kansas
- 1875 Michigan and Minnesota
- 1876 Colorado
- 1878 New Hampshire and Oregon
- 1879 Massachusetts
- 1880 Vermont, New York, and Mississippi
- 1883 Nebraska
- 1887 Arizona, South Dakota and New Jersey (Declared unconstitutional in New Jersey in 1894)
- 1888 Kentucky, for tax-paying spinsters and widows outside chartered cities
- 1889 North Dakota and Montana
- 1890 Washington and Oklahoma
- 1893 Connecticut
- 1894 Kentucky for women in cities of the second class
- 1894 Ohio
- 1898 Delaware
- 1900 Wisconsin
- 1910 New Mexico

Tax and Bond Suffrage

1878	New Hampshire.	1898	Louisiana.
1879	Massachusetts.	1901	New York.
1889	Montana.	1903	Kansas.
1894	Iowa.	1908	Michigan.

Municipal Suffrage

1887 Kansas. A similar law passed in Michigan was declared unconstitutional and discouraged such legislation till presented with presidential suffrage bills, later.

Appendix 6

DIRECTIONS FOR STATE WORK IN SUPPORT OF THE 19th AMENDMENT

1. Hold a conference of the Board of Officers, the state congressional chairman, the district congressional chairmen, the state chairman of organization, and all state organizers and two or more invited delegates from each district to meet a representative of the national board or congressional committee in private session, for the purpose of deciding ways and means for the execution of the following plans.

2. Complete the appointment of district chairman in those states where necessary; appointments to be made by state officers.

3. Complete the appointment of county chairmen (or whatever is the unit of congressional organization in your state) in territory unorganized; appointment to be made by congressional district chairmen, and ratified by the board of officers. Each congressional district chairman will then have a committee including the chairmen for counties in her district. She should add a few other women of influential standing. These should be well informed on the suffrage question and particularly on the need of a Federal Amendment. They should read all of our Federal Amendment literature as outlined on the enclosed yellow slip.

4. Be sure to push organization work in weak districts and where the senator or representative is undecided. This work may decide the whole question.

5. Set the county chairman at the task of circulating the petition hereto appended. The heads of the petition will be provided; petitioners must provide the paper. Full directions will accompany the petitions. There should be one petition for

the representative and one for each United States senator, so that each person will sign three. The aim is not quantity, but quality as judged by influence upon politics.

6. In October write the newspapers in your state and ask editorials favorable to the immediate submission of the amendment. Furnish the facts of suffrage in other lands. Better still send deputations of women and men of influence in the community to see the editors. They are busy men and do not know all that we know of the recent happenings in the big world. Give each editor our booklet "Perhaps." Ask each editor to run the petition head with space for signatures as a coupon and to print a brief request for those interested to sign and return to the newspaper, from which the county chairman will collect them.

7. Get as many clubs, groups, meetings, church societies, etc., as possible to pass a resolution calling on Congress to submit the Federal Amendment as a war measure and to send copies to their representative and two senators. Keep careful record of the number passed and forwarded.

8. In October or early November each congressional district chairman should make an appointment to see the representative from her district and should then call for a deputation of the most influential men and women to join her. A speaker from each county should make a brief appeal to the member of Congress and should present the petition from his (or her) county, the coupons from newspapers, the collection of editorials, the resolutions passed and "Perhaps." In canvassing for the petition and in the speeches made to the member, it should always be mentioned that the women of Great Britain have all suffrage rights now and that the women of nearly all Canada now have full suffrage.

9. The county petitions to the senators should be delivered in the same fashion by a deputation from each congressional district, led by the state congressional chairman, with a statement as to the number of coupons, editorials, resolutions, etc.

10. Get each county chairman to keep a copy of the most influential names on her petition and send a copy to her district chairman, to the state chairman and to the national chairman. It may be necessary to wire these persons to send letters and telegrams to their members upon emergency. A New York senator made the statement that he received ten thousand letters, postals and telegrams asking him to vote against war. That is probably a fair gauge of what we must be prepared to do on our question for *every* senator.

If your staff is too limited to do this additional work interest other women as volunteer aides. If you are short of money, beg or borrow it. You will need to follow up continually the instructions sent to chairmen. You will need to keep in touch with them in order to learn whether they are doing the work. If not, an officer or organizer must go to learn why and perhaps to find a more dependable chairman. Be sure your organization is active in every county. This plan will furnish the motive for doing it.

We shall win when and if this work is faithfully done.

Appendix 7

DIRECTIONS FOR LOBBYISTS

I. PREPARATION:
   1. Read our records of each member before calling on him. Also read biographical sketch in Congressional Directory. Records must not be taken from office.
   2. Provide yourself with a small directory. Your own representative is the best source of supply.

II. INTERVIEWING:
   1. If the member appears busy ask whether he would prefer to see you at some other time.
   2. Be courteous no matter what provocation you may seem to have to be otherwise.
   3. If possible learn the secretary's name and have a little talk with him or her. The secretary if inclined to be interested should be invited to headquarters.
   4. If the member is known to be in favor show that you realize that fact and ask him for advice and help with the rest of the delegation. This point is *very important*.
   5. Be sure to keep his *party* constantly in mind while talking to him.
   6. Be a good listener. Don't interrupt.
   7. Try to avoid prolonged or controversial argument. It is likely to confirm men in their own opinion.
   8. Do not stay so long that the member has to give the signal for departure.

9. Take every possible means to prevent a member from *committing* himself definitely *against* the Federal Amendment. This is *most important*.
10. Leave the way open for another interview if you have failed to convince him.
11. If the member is inclined to be favorable invite him and his family to headquarters.
12. Remember to hold each interview confidential. Never quote what one member has said to you to another member. It is not safe to talk of your lobby experiences before outsiders. We can never know by what route our stories may get back to the member and injure our cause with him. We cannot be too cautious in this matter.

III. REPORTS:
1. Do not make notes in offices or halls.
2. Do find opportunity to make notes on one interview before starting on another. If necessary step into the "ladies" dressing room to do this.
3. Write a full report of your interview on the same day, giving—
   a. Name and state of member
   b. *Date* and hour of interview
   c. Names of lobbyists and name of person making the report
   d. Member's argument in detail especially with view to follow-up work
   e. Any information you may glean about his family or friends that may be useful to the Washington committee
   f. Hand written report to *chairman* not later than the day following the interview.
   g. Promptness in turning in reports is most important in order that lists and polls may be kept up to date.

Appendix 8

CHRONOLOGY OF CONGRESSIONAL ACTION

1868   Passage of the 14th Amendment which introduced the word male into the Constitution

1869   First woman suffrage bill introduced into the House.

1869   Hearing on woman suffrage

1878   Introduction by Senator Sargent of the Woman Suffrage Amendment in its final form

1887   January 25, first vote in the Senate, yeas 16, nays 34, 50 voting

1914   March 19, second vote in the Senate, yeas 35, nays 34, 69 voting

1915   January 12, first vote in the House, yeas 174, nays 204, 378 voting

1917   Sept. 24, Creation of Woman Suffrage Committee in the House

1918   January 10, second vote in the House, yeas 274, nays 136, 410 voting

1918   October 1, third vote in the Senate, yeas, including pairs, 62, nays, 34

1919   February 10, fourth vote in the Senate, yeas, including pairs, 63, nays 33

1919   May 21, third vote in the House, yeas 304, nays 89

1919   June 4, fifth vote in the Senate, yeas, including pairs, 66, nays 30

1920   August 26, proclamation by the Secretary of State of the 19th Amendment

Appendix 9

AUTHORS WHO'S WHO

Mildred Adams is a well known magazine writer on current affairs. She cannot remember when she was not a feminist, and, living in California, she had the then rare felicity of casting her first vote immediately she came of age. She graduated in economics at the University of California, and her recent book "Getting and Spending" is the A.B.C. of economics. She was also the editor of "Rebel in Bombazine", Memoirs of a German feminist, and translator and editor of "Invertebrate Spain" by José Ortega y Gasset.

Gertrude Foster Brown (Mrs. Raymond) was lured away from music by the suffrage cause. After brief apprenticeship she became president of the New York State Suffrage Association, 1913-1915 and then till the victory in 1917, its chairman of organization. She has been a vice-president of the National American Woman Suffrage Association since 1917. In 1918 she went to France as general director for the Women's Overseas Hospitals, work carried on by the suffrage organizations. For many years she served on the state board of the New York League of Women Voters. From 1921 to 1931 she was the managing director of *The Woman Citizen*, successor to *The Woman's Journal*.

Penelope B. P. Huse (Mrs. Robert S.) was vice-president and later legislative chairman of the New Jersey Woman Suffrage Association, and chairman of presidential suffrage in the National American Woman Suffrage Association. In 1924 she became the executive secretary of the American Birth Control League. She worked in the National Committee for Maternal Health from 1929 for ten years, and is now assistant to the general director of the Birth Control Federation of America.

Mary Foulke Morrisson (Mrs. James) is secretary to the board of trustees of Connecticut College. Her father, William Dudley Foulke, was for many years president of the American Woman Suffrage Association. She became secretary and then president of the Chicago Woman Suffrage Association. She took a leading part in the war work of Illinois. An active Republican she seconded the nomination of Herbert Hoover at the National Republican Convention in 1920. She was an organizer of the Illinois League of Women Voters, and later its president. She has been active in the Conferences on the Cause and Cure of War, and an officer in the Institute of Pacific Relations.

Maud Wood Park was the first president of the College Equal Suffrage League, 1901-1903; secretary of the Boston Equal Suffrage Association for Good Government, 1903-1907 and 1910-1916; congressional chairman of the National American Woman Suffrage Association, 1917-1919 and the first president of the National League of Women Voters, 1920-1924. She has returned to work in the drama for which she had trained before the suffrage movement caught her, and her play, "Lucy Stone," has been widely given by stock companies and dramatic clubs.

Mary Gray Peck is a graduate of Elmira College and was graduate student of English at the University of Minnesota and at Cambridge University, England. She was for ten years assistant professor of English at the University of Minnesota. From 1910 to 1920 she devoted herself to the suffrage struggle. She has since been active in organizations working for international cooperation and peace.